'To tackle the impact of disadvantage on children [...] for area-based 'cradle to career' strategies – exten[...] to involve schools, other agencies like health an[...] of charities, social enterprises and businesses in integrated community-based services. Doug Martin's excellent book provides an essential resource to help make this happen. Doug enables understanding in his sharp review of the history that brought extended schools. The insightful penultimate chapter develops an understanding of extended schools – of what they achieve and what they are for. And in between are many detailed and useful case studies. For anyone wanting to develop more integrated community schooling – this is a go-to text.'

Liz Todd, Professor of Educational Inclusion, University of Newcastle

'The development of extended schools in England during the 2000s was a remarkable educational experiment of international significance. Yet it has been too little studied by researchers and its implications remain under-explored. This important book reports one of the few studies we have of how the extended schools agenda was actually implemented – what difficulties were encountered and what opportunities opened up. We urgently need to rethink the relationships between schools, children and communities, and this book helps us do just that. It should be read by anyone who believes in the wider possibilities of schooling.'

Alan Dyson, Professor of Education, University of Manchester

'This book provides an impressive and insightful consideration of the field and and provides a very strong analysis concerning how we develop and connect learning relationships to issues of social justice, professionalism, social capital, strength-based working, and community-based support. In revisiting how we fund state schools Martin encourages us to look beyond short-term ideas and consider how we can specifically address and remove the barriers to learning for children and young people.'

John Davis, Professor of Childhood Inclusion, University of Edinburgh

Whatever Happened to Extended Schools?

With love to Ingrid, Jenny, and Sue, and to Evie, Maisie, Max, Georgia, and Zac for reminding me of the importance of childhood.

Whatever Happened to Extended Schools?

The story of an ambitious education project

Doug Martin

First published in 2016 by the UCL Institute of Education Press, 20 Bedford Way, London WC1H 0AL

www.ucl-ioe-press.com

©2016 Doug Martin

British Library Cataloguing in Publication Data:
A catalogue record for this publication is available from the British Library

ISBNs
978-1-78277-049-7 (paperback)
978-1-78277-184-5 (PDF eBook)
978-1-78277-185-2 (ePub eBook)
978-1-78277-186-9 (Kindle eBook)

All rights reserved. No part of this publication may be reproduced, stored in a retrieval system, or transmitted in any form or by any means, electronic, mechanical, photocopying, recording or otherwise, without the prior permission of the copyright owner.

Every effort has been made to trace copyright holders and to obtain their permission for the use of copyright material. The publisher apologizes for any errors or omissions and would be grateful if notified of any corrections that should be incorporated in future reprints or editions of this book.

The opinions expressed in this publication are those of the author and do not necessarily reflect the views of the UCL Institute of Education.

Typeset by Quadrant Infotech (India) Pvt Ltd
Printed by CPI Group (UK) Ltd, Croydon, CR0 4YY

Front cover: Bubbles Photolibrary/Alamy Stock Photo.
Back cover: Mark Spowart/Alamy Stock Photo.

Contents

List of tables	viii
Acknowledgements	ix
About the author	ix
Foreword by Peter Moss	x
Introduction	1
1. Changing approaches to English schooling	9
2. Orpintown: Extended Schools and a market town	32
3. Gadley: Extended Schools building a new sense of community	53
4. Hayfield: Extended Schools legitimizing schools' approach	73
5. Newtown: Extended Schools and a community rebuilding itself	89
6. Extended Schools: Contribution to the schooling discourse	108
7. Looking ahead: The school in 2030	136
Appendix 1: National policy publications and local partnership developments in relation to Extended Schools development in England	151
Appendix 2: Key developments in Extended Schools at local partnership level	154
References	157
Index	162

List of tables

Table 2.1 Orpintown Partnership governance arrangements

Table 2.2 Orpintown Partnership Universal Services subgroup

Table 2.3 Orpintown Partnership Targeted Family Services subgroup

Table 2.4 Orpintown Partnership: a selection of services developed

Table 3.1 Gadley Schools Partnership Trust Board

Table 3.2 Gadley Extended Schools Board

Table 3.3 Gadley Extended Schools Board: a selection of services developed

Table 4.1 Hayfield Schools: multi-professional team

Table 4.2 Hayfield Extended Schools: a selection of services developed

Table 4.3 Hayfield Extended Schools Breakfast Business meeting

Table 5.1 Newtown Extended Schools Board

Table 5.2 Newtown Extended Schools Partnership Group

Table 5.3 Newtown Extended Schools: a selection of services developed

Acknowledgements

I would like to thank all those that gave of their time to participate in this research and acknowledge how many of them displayed a deep seated passion to improve the lives of children and families. I would also like to express my thanks to a number of academics that advised and guided me through this research and with the development of this publication, and in particular Peter Moss.

About the author

Dr Doug Martin is Senior Lecturer in Education and Childhood at Leeds Beckett University. His career has spanned the education and welfare sectors of public services in the UK, including roles in health, social care, community education, and schools. At a strategic level, he has led change programmes such as those associated with Every Child Matters and national policy development. He works in a voluntary capacity with young people and as trustee of voluntary agencies and as a school governor. His academic research continues to cut across organizational and professional boundaries with the aim to better understand why services conceptualize children through a fragmented lens. His work has led to policy development and new ways of working across children and adult services and schools.

Foreword

Education in England over the last 30 years, since the Education Reform Act of 1988, has been dominated by four themes: governance, choice, regulation and performance. Local authority control has been replaced by self-government and, with the rise of academies and free schools, a direct contractual role for central government. Parents have been given, at least on paper, increased say over which school their children attend; a national curriculum and a new national inspection agency have been introduced and endlessly wrangled over, while examinations have proliferated, with endless picking over the performance of both children and schools. What has emerged is a particular idea of schools as exam factories (Coffield and Williamson, 2011) judged predominantly on their productivity for pass rates and grade levels, and as businesses, autonomous bodies competing in a market place for children, their primary relationship increasingly focused on individual parent-consumers, and overseen by a distant government and its agent, Ofsted. Underpinning these developments has been what Michael Apple has described as 'a new alliance that is exerting leadership in educational policies and educational reform' (Apple, 2005: 20): neoliberalism and neoconservatism, backed by the committed support of a particular faction of the middle class, professional and managerial groups that have thrived in the new climate of competition, measurement, managerialism, and technical practice.

Something strange happened for a few years at the start of the century, complicating this picture of seemingly inevitable movement towards a new education regime. Something that potentially had the capacity to disturb and disrupt, to open up a democratic politics of education where the taken-for-granted is no longer so, where the technical 'what works?' is replaced by the political 'where to?', and where genuinely political questions are publicly discussed, questions such as what is the meaning of education, what is its purpose, and what is our image of the school. What caused this window of opportunity was the New Labour government's espousal of the Extended School, first tentatively in a 'Full Service Extended School pilot', introduced in 2002, then in a comprehensive policy commitment, announcing in 2005 that all publicly-funded schools would become Extended Schools: schools whose explicit purpose was more than just exams and whose relationships extended beyond parents to their whole local communities – schools as multi-purpose institutions for all citizens. All this was undertaken within the broader context of 'Every Child Matters', a huge policy initiative launched in 2003 that set broad common aims for all children's services, established new universal institutions (not only Extended Schools but Children's Centres for younger children and their families), and placed responsibility for all children and families within a single government ministry, the Department for Children, Schools and Families, whose very name spoke of a far broader ambition and a much wider perspective.

For those of us working in the field of children, schools, and families during these few years, there was a strange mismatch between the broad sweep, huge ambitions and rapid momentum of government policy and apparent public unawareness, at least of the big picture. Parents may have used Children's Centres or been aware that something was changing at their children's schools, but I suspect that very few would have realized this was part of a far larger programme and most would probably have looked blank if asked about the 'Every Child Matters agenda'. This agenda never became the subject of a high profile, public politics. And though there was great growth in services, and much activity by policy-makers and practitioners, the roots were shallow, unable to resist a new government in 2010, one of whose first acts was to replace the 'Department for Children, Schools and Families' with the 'Department for Education'. Political inclination, combined with austerity, meant the party was well and truly over; the window of opportunity was closed.

It is, of course, possible to be too nostalgic about the New Labour government's burst of activity, and to lose perspective. New Labour may have espoused a new, broad policy agenda, including Extended Schools, but it did not abandon the other recurrent themes of governance, choice, regulation, and performance. In schools, the 'Every Child Matters' agenda sat, perhaps uncomfortably, alongside a continuing standards agenda. Change was hurried and frenetic, and very much top down, pressed forward amid a constant blizzard of Whitehall directions and requirements; the desire to govern, regulate and control was always likely to overwhelm the possibilities for emancipation, participation, and local experimentation. Complex and long-term changes were compressed into a few years. The opportunity to open up and build a democratic politics of education, involving the wider public in debate about political questions, was eschewed, the potential for renewal not fully realized. And yet, despite these caveats, I think that something important was being attempted, something that might have led to a better life for children, families, and communities; something that might have opened up the possibility for new thinking about and

Foreword

understanding of education and schools, moving from narrower to broader interpretations and stimulating new understandings of professionalism in children's services.

It is in this context that Doug Martin's book is so important. At a time when the memory of Every Child Matters and Extended Schools is fading fast, when the policy agenda has returned with a vengeance to an exclusive concern with governance, choice, regulation, and performance, when the school seems more than ever to be viewed by government as primarily a business selling exam results – we should remember Extended Schools. And do more than remember: to reflect upon their experience, to assess the challenges they faced and what they achieved, and to consider how, someday, we might build on this experience to create education-in-its-broadest-sense and schools that are public spaces in the public domain and public resources – not only for children and parents, but for the whole community, genuinely public schools. This book, based on doctoral research undertaken in four schools and communities, has a vital role to play in such work of remembrance and reflection, giving a vivid insight into an ambitious education project and using that to build an imaginative portrayal of how an Extended School of the future might be.

Emeritus Professor Peter Moss
UCL Institute of Education
University College London

References

Apple, M. (2005) 'Education, markets and an audit culture', *Critical Quarterly* 47 (1–2), 11–29.

Coffield, F., and Williamson, B. (2011) *From Exam Factories to Communities of Discovery: The democratic route*. London: Institute of Education.

Introduction

For the last 30 years much discussion has taken place in England about schooling and education with a primary focus upon performance and governance rather the meaning and potentiality of education and schools. But for a brief period in the last decade attention shifted towards the latter, perhaps as a result of the continued strong correlation between disadvantage and educational achievement. During this brief interlude different, more fundamental discussions started to emerge such as: what is education? What are schools for? And how does schooling relate to the wider community? This debate, when combined with an historical legacy of schooling set within a pseudo-market place, saw education and schooling briefly at a crossroads both at national level and within local communities. The research that this book is based upon took place within schools and their communities from 2006 to 2010 when these critical discussions were being played out triggered by the implementation of the Extended School policy. The research continued until 2014 as English education policy returned to a more familiar discussion concerning school performance and governance through a period that became labelled as a 'return to traditional educational values' (Gove, 2010). This book provides unique insights into how schools and their recently found partners responded to these fundamental, shifting interpretations of what is education and the role of schools.

The research initially developed as a result of a PhD begun in 2005 that was linked to my professional interest in schooling, children, their families and communities. I had worked for many years within inner-city communities and an overwhelming view of many families was that their school experiences were of little relevance to their lives. Also as a strategic manager I gained a growing interest in the national agenda of 'joining up' services, resulting from New Labour's policy development in the late 1990s. Examples of these policies included the establishment of youth-offender teams, the Connexions strategy, Sure Start Local Programmes, and the Every Child Matters policy. Each of these policies aimed to develop multi-agency approaches fuelled by an increasing emphasis upon early intervention and prevention, as opposed to the dominant deficit modelling of service provision. By deficit modelling I refer to my professional experiences of waiting until something had 'gone wrong' with a child or their family's life, followed by intervention that is often too late to put right the harm. But intriguingly most of these multi-agency or multi-professional developments appeared to have an emphasis on the work outside the framework of the English schooling system. Schools and medical General Practitioners (GPs) are the cornerstone of the welfare state providing universal services to a vast majority of children, but schools stood firmly outside a reform agenda in terms of an emphasis on 'joined-up working', 'joined-up thinking', early intervention, and prevention. Schools appeared to be trapped within an ethos of performance linked to the testing of children and parental choice.

The Full Service Extended School pilots of 2002 followed by the Extended Schools agenda of 2005 hinted at providing ways through which local children and young people's services might be more closely linked to local schooling. Perhaps this could herald the commencement of a new discourse for education, after many years of fixation on autonomy and performance? Having worked in both the welfare and education fields of public service I was well versed in the professionalism of front-line staff, middle managers, and strategic leaders. Common across almost all provision I engaged with was how services were overwhelmingly set within a culture focused upon their host organization and organizational measures of success linked to deep-seated understanding of professional interests. The latter, often fostered through professional training and the formation of communities of practice, linked to professional identity. After leading developments in children and young people's services emerging from the New Labour policy machinery I understood how rigidly the professionalism of those working in schools was also framed. And, I observed how some local authority leaders and professionals alike sought to 'ride out' the potential impact of major policy shifts; an example being the Every Child Matters agenda and evidence of organizational and professional resistance to radical change it provoked.

Working in this environment triggered a PhD research study that spanned the second half of the New Labour years from 2005 to 2010. I wanted to understand how the newly unveiled 'Extended Schools: access to opportunities and services for all: a prospectus' (DfES, 2005) would impact upon both leaders and professionals working in schools and in broader community-based services. And, as someone working on both national and local policy agendas linked to Every Child Matters, I observed how central government was becoming increasingly frustrated by local authorities and their perceived inability to successfully engage with the Change for Children programme; this view was later spelt out by a Children's Minister in a research interview. I surmised that perhaps New Labour saw localized transformation as more achievable through further devolution of change to school leaders and local professionals working in communities through a policy development that asked them to form new local partnerships. Perhaps this was an experiment that could shift the discourse of education and in particular English schooling from the fixation upon performance and governance to a more fundamental debate concerning what education is and what the twenty-first-century school might be like?

Returning to the original aim of the research, this was to better understand how new local partnerships were being constructed by school leaders in response to the New Labour policy set out in 2005. There seemed to be opportunities for professional interplay between the universal services of schools and more targeted community-based services. Extended Schools asked school leaders to develop a 'Core Offer' of services (DfES, 2006). The Core Offer consisted of: out of school hours activities for children, childcare provision, parenting support, adult learning opportunities, and swift and easy referral of children to more specialist services. When schools were asked to respond to this new agenda by central government it represented a change of direction. Schools were enjoying the autonomy provided by the 1988 Education Reform Act and were also in competition with each other in terms of parental choice. Providing these new services entailed schools looking outside their gates to begin to potentially work with other schools in their locality, and also children and young people's services based in their communities. It also involved schools refreshing or re-establishing their relationship with their local authority (LA).

Cummings *et al.* (2011: 14) retrospectively describe the Extended Schools policy drive as 'a remarkable experiment'. The research was not afforded this hindsight, therefore the depth to which the policy was to question existing leadership approaches to schooling and the leadership of broader service provision; nor was the depth to which it would question the professionalism for all that engaged with it understood. However, a pilot research project suggested that policy may have a fundamental impact upon the schools, children, and young people's workforces as had other contemporary experimental policy strands such as the Full Service Schools pilots. This piloting activity also served to verify that through a longitudinal PhD study there may be the potential for significant new knowledge and understandings to materialize.

Extended Schools appeared to present a new opportunity and permit schools to engage with a much broader agenda than that of performance and governance rooted within the 1988 Education Reform Act. Moss and Haydon (2008) described schools set within this performance agenda as engaging with education in its narrower sense. Would the implementation of Extended Schools bring about a shift in school professionalism towards education in its broader sense? The latter promised to locate schools within the context of learning that engages with broader understandings of pupils and their lives outside the classroom. By using this concept of education, the research sought to understand the changing nature of leadership and professionalism. Were schools shifting from the status of education in its narrower sense to one of education in its broader sense? What would this entail for leaders and professionals working in the schools and children and young people's workforce?

An ambitious research project was established, which sought to take a longitudinal approach to capture change resulting from the implementation of the Extended Schools policy in four diverse communities in England. The methodology involved engagement with local residents who were also usually parents of children in local schools, front-line practitioners from a variety of community-based services, primary and secondary school-based staff including their leaders, local authority and health service managers, strategic figures, and, at national level, policy makers and political leaders. The latter included two New Labour Children's Ministers covering the period 2003 to 2009, influential in the progression of policy that served to bring together schools with community-based services, as were two national policy makers. These national figures set school leaders on a journey of experimentation, which not only caused new relationships to be formed with local authorities but, perhaps inadvertently, gave school leaders permission to explore new possibilities for English schooling itself.

What seemed at first to be a straightforward investigation of Extended Schools policy implementation quickly turned into research concerning a fundamental revision of state schooling and broader community-based services, as Gordon Brown became Prime Minister and renamed the Department for Education and Skills (DfES) as the Department for Children, Schools and Families (DCSF). The thrust of policy through the Children's Plan (DCSF, 2007a) shifted the focus of the Every Child Matters flagship policy from LAs to these emerging local Extended Schools partnerships. State schools were being directed towards becoming hubs of services for their local community through the twenty-first-century school policy drive (DCSF, 2008). But as with all policy implementation, especially experimental policy as this was, there are those leaders and practitioners that embrace and work with change and those with a tendency to ignore it and hope it will go away. This research benefited from working with four diverse partnerships that for one reason or another drove forward Extended Schools developments within their community and which provided unique insights into the potential for schools to become positioned centrally within their community.

A second, lighter touch, phase of this study extended the longitudinal research to cover the policy developments of the Conservative and Liberal Democrat Coalition of 2010 (referred to here as the Coalition). But, unfortunately, unlike New Labour, despite numerous requests for Coalition Ministers to participate in this research, all approaches were firmly declined. This included former Ministers that were no longer serving in the DfE due to reshuffles between 2010 to 2014. So this study continued, though more limited in depth, compared to phase one, to include observations of local meetings, interviews with leaders and front-line staff, and ongoing documentary analysis.

The return, as the Coalition defined it, to 'traditional educational values' was accompanied by the move of the government to take further centralized control of schooling through the extension of the academy programme. But there was also a strong sentiment held by the Coalition to disregard much of New Labour's policy. In 2010 following the General Election government websites posted disclaimers stating that policy featured may not be the policy of the Coalition. A further shift in the positioning of LAs, in the context of children and young people's services and schools, saw New Labour's structured central focus of responsibility for the delivery of local integrated welfare and education services for children being dropped. At national level the aspirations of achieving a single coherent workforce strategy (CWDC, 2009) across all services with common values and understandings was also disregarded by the Coalition. There was a loss of emphasis on Extended Schools developments as school policy reverted to the discourse of governance and performance. Between 2010 and 2014 this second phase of the research continued, in the same four communities that had successfully engineered new, local partnerships, to map how new policy impacted upon their development.

Hence the research covers almost eight years of shifting policy, including the progressive experimentation of New Labour, whilst maintaining the neoliberal traits of competition between schools and the stark shift of the Coalition towards policy set within a neoliberal framework, but now accompanied by severe reductions in public spending never witnessed before in England. Appendix 1 provides a summary of the key policy milestones from 1999 to 2014. The freedom afforded to this research to respond to changing policy, coupled with the motivation to gain understandings of the complex journey on which these partnerships were set, provides a unique insight into schooling and community-based services and the changing demands made upon them by both New Labour and the Coalition. At times the pace of change and the complexity of issues tackled threatened to overwhelm the project, but the potential to learn from data that was captured, the ongoing analysis, and a commitment to seek understanding of these issues kept the project on track, revealing insights into English schooling and its relationships with community-based services that also often work with the same children in the same community.

This book captures a selection of the key insights gained from the research. It aims to engage the reader in a debate about the positioning of state funded schooling in England and how it could be differently positioned to improve outcomes for all children, families and their community. In doing so, it also engages the reader with the fundamental questions: what is education for and what is the potential of schooling in a post-industrial society?

A review of the historical research that informed this study, about schools and their relationship with their community, revealed a raft of work that could be categorized as sitting with the community schooling movement, of which there was a strong tradition largely pre-dating the 1988 Education Reform Act. More contemporary specific research was conducted into the Full Service Extended School pilots and Extended Schools agendas by a team mainly involving the Universities of Manchester and Newcastle, which was initially funded by DfES to evaluate the implementation of policy development. From this team a range of updates were published by Cummings *et al.* from 2005, which has informed this research. Dyson and Todd further published specific research papers with reference to Extended Schools across the period 2002 to 2010. Additionally, the National College of School Leadership commissioned research led by Leadbeater and Mongon from 2008 to 2010, which culminated with a publication in 2012. But, the research that is featured in this book is unique in the scope of its engagement with a range of players, from a diversity of communities that sought to implement the Extended Schools policy.

Chapter 1 outlines a selection of policy developments that have contributed to our understanding of the English schooling system. A brief history of free universal education will include the developments over the last century of the positioning of schools in relation to their community. It examines the implications of the marketization of state education rooted in the rise of neoliberalism, and accompanied by an emphasis on control of the neoconservatives in the 1980s driven by the New Right. An outline of New Labour policy development across 1997–2010 in relation to schooling is followed by an account of the new policy emphasis of the Coalition of 2010, involving the myth of the golden days of English schooling of the 1950s linked to a sentiment of 'traditional educational values'. Effectively local Extended Schools developments became entangled within a refreshed focus on education in its narrower sense propagated by the Coalition coupled with further centralization of education accompanied by severe reductions in public spending. But, although the Coalition cited the USA and Sweden as having developed models of schooling that may aid the repositioning of English schooling globally, an insight into other models of schools will be outlined and in particular ones that aim to reduce intergenerational low levels of educational achievement also adopted by these countries.

Chapters 2, 3, 4, and 5 comprise the four individual case-studies that emerged through this research. Appendix 2 provides a summary of the key sequences of events that took place in these four partnerships. The ethical framework through which this research was conducted involved providing pseudonyms for LAs, schools, their communities, and organizations that contributed to data generation, to protect the identities of participants and the organizations or communities to which they belonged. Chapter 2 focuses upon a market town setting, Orpintown, where a high school and a collection of primary schools developed a local partnership in response to LA pressure. Chapter 3 concerns a partnership formed by Gadley high school, which immediately saw that Extended Schools provided them with new possibilities of engaging with their community. This community had a deep historical sense of identity forged by the coalmining industry and was in search of a new post-industrial identity as Extended Schools emerged locally. Both Orpintown and Gadley partnerships are sited within Eastfield LA. This LA successfully transformed its economy towards the end of the last century from one based upon heavy industry to an economy mixed with new service industries. As such Eastfield had overcome the worst of economic restructuring that blighted the UK in the 1980s and was a fairly wealthy community but with pockets of deprivation found within its core. Orpintown and Gadley were now commuter areas seemingly being engulfed by a fairly prosperous city.

Chapters 4 and 5 are concerned with partnerships established in Farrington LA. This LA was very different to Eastfield LA as it comprised small towns, some challenged by the shift from an economy based upon manufacturing to one post-industrially based and numerous rural villages. These villages were largely prosperous and formed commuter areas for three major cities in neighbouring LAs. Hayfield, featured in Chapter 4, is one of these rural communities with an air of confidence and prosperity across a collection of villages. But one village was considered to be amongst the few pockets of rural deprivation sited locally. Chapter 5, the final case-study, focuses upon Newtown, a community that had lost confidence in itself, suffered from high levels of unemployment and benefit dependency. It was also subject to families new to England settling, but it was noted that these families often quickly moved on to more prosperous communities.

Chapter 6 engages with the three key themes that emerged from the analysis of data generated by this research, which are:

- schools coming together
- schools discovering the community and its services
- schools and community-based services developing new forms of mutual professionalism.

The original research aimed to gain insights into how practitioners and leaders came together to develop the Extended Schools Core Offer. But as the research continued, because it was neither restricted by time or funder's requirements to produce specific outcomes, it was able to respond with great fluidity to policy changes as they arose. This chapter will also discuss the conditions or environment that led to a new localized mutual professionalism being constructed within all of these Extended Schools partnerships.

The concluding chapter dares to challenge current policy approaches and the acceptance, both at strategic and practitioner levels, that there are no alternatives to present positioning of English schooling. Indeed there are alternatives to the contemporary acceptance that education and other services for children, young people, and families must be set within the currently accepted norm of the neoliberal/neoconservative frame, which presently pervades public services in many western societies. By using the understandings gained through the research of the conditions and environment that fostered the development of the approaches local leaders took to construct new, localized, multi-professional partnerships, it will look into the future potential of education and schooling.

Chapter 1
Changing approaches to English schooling

Introduction

This chapter will explore a broad range of policy relevant to the research and help set the context in which the fieldwork took place. The research tracked the development of Extended Schools, which cut across a diverse range of professional and organizational boundaries, in order to gain insights and understandings into a challenging policy as it was developed by New Labour. As the research commenced, in 2006, English schooling was framed within a construct of education developed through the promotion of neoliberal and neoconservative approaches to public services, a legacy of the New Right; leaders and practitioners found themselves working in and with schools set in competition with each other. This was then the accepted paradigm and it seemed no alternative could possibly lead to the improved education of children. But a historical account of the development of English schooling demonstrates that this understanding was not always the case. Schooling was embedded within local democratic processes of public services for over 80 years prior to the 1988 Education Reform Act and it involved much more than teaching within the classroom.

Perhaps we can learn from this rich history. Improving the education of our children involves much more than the contemporary internalized technical processes resulting from schools in competition with each other through utilization of simplistic measures. The correlation between children's attainment and family income and wealth is not a new phenomenon either (Cummings *et al.*, 2011). Perhaps there is a link between the narrowness of the present school improvement measures, interschool competition, and a continued failure of English schooling to tackle low levels of educational achievement in disadvantaged communities?

New Labour at the turn of the millennium, while maintaining the New Right's approach to schooling, started to experiment with the system in response to their social justice agenda. This brief interlude was played out firstly through the Full Service Extended School piloting activity and followed by the Extended Schools policy, which entailed considerations of children as more than pupils. This national policy direction abruptly closed with the Coalition government of 2010, marking a return to a New Right approach towards schooling and other public services. In 2010 the English schooling system was apparently falling behind other countries and in order to put this right the Coalition sought to learn from other countries, in particular USA and Sweden. The final section of this chapter investigates models of schooling adopted by these countries that present alternatives to those selected by the Coalition as solutions to the problems faced by English schooling.

The English schooling system and changing relations with the community

Schooling 1870 to 1988

The Industrial Revolution and the Victorian era that followed impacted heavily on English communities. Life changed dramatically and intergenerational experiences based upon rural life were broken as families migrated to urban centres in search of employment. An assortment of schools developed in these cities and towns sponsored by philanthropists, communitarians, and faith organizations. Perhaps the most notable of these was Robert Owen who pioneered the construction of a new community approach in Scotland inclusive of childcare, schooling, and health services for their workers (Donnachie, 2000). The 1870 Education Act is attributed with the establishment of free compulsory elementary education in England but this legislation in reality brought together the existing range of ad hoc schooling (Mortimore, 2013). The 1902 Education Act introduced the role of local authorities as managers responsible for local schools by abolishing the 2,568 School Boards that had grown over a 30-year period. The 328 Local Education Authorities (LEAs) established through the merger of School Boards were based within existing local democratic structures of borough and county councils (Mongon and Leadbetter, 2012). Responsibility for education remained closely linked to these recognized democratic bodies for over 70 years. 'The 1944 Education Act consolidated the approach of a national system of schooling locally administered' through LEAs (Ainley, 2001: 458) and commenced the expansion of a system of free schooling to include the secondary sector (Garratt and Forrester, 2012).

Despite the continued investment in schooling in the post-war years, James Callaghan, Labour Prime Minister from 1976 to 1979, in his Ruskin speech in Oxford in 1976 started to question the quality of governance arrangements of English schools and in particular the apparent failure of poorer children to succeed within the present system (Department of Education and Science/Welsh Office, 1977). This 1970s critique closely resonates with statements made by the leadership of New Labour as they came to power some 30 years later. Perhaps Callaghan was diverted from his mission to improve schooling by the overwhelming economic issues the country faced. LEAs remained in control of local educational planning until halfway through Margaret Thatcher's premiership (1979 to 1990) when she was reminded by advisors that English schooling had remained largely untouched by her reform agenda (*The Guardian*, 2014).

A review of the history of the nature of relationships between schools and their communities in England between 1870 and 1988 demonstrates that, rather than being a policy-orientated approach, it has been more one of personalities. Jeffs (1999) notes the work of Henry Morris, the Chief Education Officer for Cambridgeshire, in the 1920s which at that time comprised poor rural communities. The 'village college' model he proposed positioned schools as the hubs of their community. Morris (1924) suggested this would draw together existing social and educational elements to forge a new relationship. This principle was also adopted by other mainly rural LEAs in response to socially changing factors (Cummings *et al.*, 2011). Boroughs in London, where social changes resulted in high levels of poverty, accompanied by unemployment in the post-war years, particularly in communities linked with the docks, also considered their schools as central community resources. Inner-city London schools became centres for family engagement and not just the teaching of children (Franklin, 2009).

The Plowden Report (CACE, 1967) echoed some of these ideas and promoted a much broader role for schools than that of teaching children. The report recommended that schools should embrace other public service areas such as social care and health services for children. A new emphasis on the home–school relationship was cited as a way to improve the education of children from disadvantaged communities, involving greater emphasis on parental participation. Indeed this issue of the poor performance of disadvantaged children in the schooling system is not one confined to contemporary England, but one highlighted by successive governments since the 1960s as a reprehensible stain on English schooling. Structural examples constructed in response to Plowden included schools and the community working much more closely together. Communities where improvement in educational achievement was an issue were identified as Education Priority Areas (EPAs) (Cummings *et al.*, 2011), an attempt to develop policy leading to closer school and community relationships involving broader considerations of children than those set within the classroom. Despite this community-based approach being cast aside relatively quickly, EPA principles were rediscovered by New Labour as they started to experiment with schooling some 30 years later through the establishment of Education Action Zones (EAZs), focused on inner-city disadvantaged communities.

Returning to Cambridgeshire and the legacy of Morris (Piper, 2006), and following the publication of Plowden, the County Council established a number of community schools in 1975, which were expected to pursue a wider role than that of the education of children in their care (Cambridgeshire LEA, 1976). Midwinter (1973) highlighted the work of schools in Liverpool, discussing this community-based approach to schooling and how each school's management regime should broaden to include the community and wider service provision. Piper (2006) describes how similar work developed in Birmingham, Coventry, and Leicestershire in the 1980s. The idea of Extended Schools is certainly nothing new, nor the twenty-first-century school announced by New Labour in 2007 (DCSF, 2007b). The Children's Plan (DCSF, 2007a) outlined a new and challenging role for schools with every school working in partnership with local agencies so that they became concerned with broader engagement with children.

The relationship between schools and their community is therefore part of a story that constantly shifts. But it is consistently underpinned by an understanding that in more disadvantaged communities this broader engagement has the potential to improve the educational achievement of children.

Schooling 1988–1997

State schooling in England developed under the guidance of central government since its inception in the 1870s and from 1902 with an emphasis on local planning and management through LAs until 1988. During this time a consensus existed across major political parties supporting the development and expansion of free schooling (Howlett, 2013). Callaghan, as discussed earlier, voiced discontent with the English schooling system in his Ruskin Speech (Department of Education and Science/Welsh Office, 1977) and called for improved schooling for children living in disadvantaged communities. As global economic problems loomed higher on the political and social agenda this post-war settlement across the political spectrum was increasingly challenged by the strengthening of the New Right (Clarke and Newman, 1997).

Garratt and Forrester (2012) describe the New Right movement, driven by Thatcher in the UK and Reagan in the USA across the 1980s, as a coalescing of neoliberal and neoconservative philosophies. These are two distinct political rationales with few overlapping characteristics and appear contrary in nature. Brown (2006) suggests that neoliberalism is primarily about free-market economic policies coupled with a form of political rationality that positions the market as the norm through law and social policy. Thus citizens assume the mantle of economic actors in every sphere of life, with public services consisting of entrepreneurs and consumers set within an environment of 'self-care'. Conversely Brown describes neoconservatives as an alliance of different interests, most commonly linked to religions, that construct authoritarian philosophies seeking a strong state allied with corporations. They reject the vulgarity of mass culture and position themselves with religious crusades, often fundamental Christianity, and praise older forms or traditions of family values with a strong stand against the seemingly crumbling morals of western countries.

The emergence of this neoliberal and neoconservative alliance commenced a fundamental shift in the repositioning of the individual as a central player within western society. The individual operating as a consumer within the market place of public services replaced the collectivist sentiment of post-war British society (Winlow and Hall, 2013). However, the discourse concerning neoliberalism and contemporary society is a complex one. Shamir reveals he:

> ... treat[s] neoliberalism as a complex and incoherent, unstable and even contradictory set of practices that are organized around a certain imagination of the 'market' as a basis for the universalization of market-based social relationships, with the corresponding penetrations in almost every aspect of our lives.
> (Shamir, 2008: 3)

The 1988 Education Reform Act, of which much is written, introduced the Local Management of Schools that saw funding passed from LEAs to schools. This move was accompanied by other policy changes that resulted in increased national standardization and more central government control (Ball, 2013). These new measures included the introduction of the National Curriculum, the formation of a new inspectorate (Ofsted), regular inspections of individual schools and Standardized Assessment Testing (SATs) (Mortimore, 2013). A curious mix of delegation of power directly to schools combined with a trend towards increased national prescription of statutory education formed the basis upon which English schooling was to operate in future, which served to marginalize LAs, indeed until the present day. These reforms were underpinned by a new philosophy that influenced the educator and educational professionalism. Headteachers and governing bodies worked with an increasing sense of autonomy within a competitive pseudo-market (Ball, 2013). But these institutions were not set free in a true market where consumers purchase education. Instead there was a controlled market created and funded by government, whereby checks and balances remained in place through government funding linked to a growing trend towards competition between schools. The market in schooling was based upon parental choice of publicly funded schooling, where schools were funded upon places chosen by parents using measures of success involving newly introduced school league tables, as the press referred to them, and judgements based upon each individual school's Ofsted inspection report (Whitty, 2002). The New Right public-service reforms of the 1980s saw families increasingly becoming cast as consumers within a market of public services. In terms of English schooling the 1988 Education Reform Act introduced the notion of competition directly into the local school, its leadership and workforce. The legislation shifted the mindset of the educator from that of a public servant to one required, through the introduction a quasi-market place in schooling (also sometimes referred to as a pseudo-market) to now consider parents and their choice of school as an indicator of success, combined with the national testing results and inspection reports (Ball, 2013).

The neoconservative aspect of this coalescence that formed the New Right's approach involved the adoption of a philosophy deeply committed to traditional morality, linked with social authority (Apple, 2001). In broader policy terms this played out through moralizing about those individuals and families dependent upon the state. The New Right successfully broke the post-war political consensus that included the acceptance of full employment as central to British society; unemployment was viewed, by politicians that bought into this post-war consensus, as unfortunate and those that were unemployed were victims of a failure by society to fulfil its ambition of full employment. But neoconservatives in the 1980s promoted the view that the unemployed were an underclass, of their own doing, through feckless decision-making and hapless lifestyles (Winlow and Hall, 2013). And Apple (2004: 175), an observer of both USA and UK schooling, describes neoconservatives in the context of education policy as: 'deeply committed to establishing tighter mechanisms of control over knowledge, morals and materials through national and state curricula and national and state mandated testing'.

Further to this Apple (2009) argues that marketization engages with a culture of incentives for people motivated by their personal gain, as opposed to one of collective responsibility. This opens up schools to criticism of their shared collectivist values, historically linked to their role as educators and has resulted, through a combination of neoliberalism and neoconservative philosophy, to the approach of schools changing, including the professionalism of the leadership and its workforce, as a result of competition replacing collectivist principles.

There is much written about the 1988 Education Reform Act and this is not a place to delve too deeply into the detailed implications for schooling over the two and a half decades of its implementation. However, a fundamental impact upon the schools that took part in this research was that the implementation of neoliberal and neoconservative policy shifted these schools, and therefore the education they provided, from one of a public asset embedded within local democratic processes to one of a commodity to be selected or rejected by parents. Schooling was framed as a choice of something to be consumed within the market place, and not as it had been, a local service for the community. The selection or spurning of schools occurred within a framework of a national set curriculum, with pupil success measured by standardized tests, accompanied by judgements made by a national inspectorate, that were transmitted to parents through reports drawn upon individual schools. Schools became autonomous bodies with a decreasing accountability to local democratic processes, while falling under the influence of an increasingly stronger central state and detachment from their community.

Fielding and Moss, of this repositioning of schooling, warn:

> … the consequences of this alliance of ideologies [neoliberal and neoconservative] and the interest groups [sections of the middle class] with ensuring techno-managerialist dominance of education are serious. Politics and ethics are drained, leaving education as an economic commodity, education as a source of profit, economic performance as education's prime goal. Any idea of education as a public responsibility and site of democratic and ethical practice is replaced by education as a production process, a site of technical practice commodity governed by a means/end logic.
>
> Fielding and Moss (2011: 23)

At the front line of schooling this marketization caused school leaders, as we will see, to look internally within their individual organizations and their school's workforce and to supply technical processes through which to improve their school's positioning.

Schooling 1997–2010

When New Labour came to power in 1997, schools were well versed in the art of working within a market place and in many cases, if not all, became increasingly separated from the processes of local democracy and the community itself. Documents recently released by government, for example 'Education without LEAs' marked 'secret' (*The Guardian*, 2014), demonstrate how the New Right's aim was to detach all schools from any links with local democracy. In effect an ambition to bring about the conversion of state schools to academies funded by and accountable to central government (*The Guardian*, 2014). Although they did not succeed with this ambition, in a relatively short period of nine years leading to New Labour taking office, the combined ethos of neoliberal and neoconservative approaches had become deeply embedded within the English schooling system. In terms of competition between schools 'there is no alternative' (Winlow and Hall, 2013: 18) had become the New Right mantra, and Apple's (2001) critique of this stance to schooling was one seemingly portrayed as one of 'common sense'.

The year 1997 marked a new era of public service modernization (Blair, 2010). Schools were central to this agenda, which Tony Blair, Prime Minister from 1997 to 2007, described as an 'unprecedented crusade to raise standards' (1999:15). Blair, like his predecessor, Callaghan, saw education as a key lever to improving social mobility and after 18 years of New Right philosophy held a view that schooling, while improving the education of the middle classes, was still failing large sections of English society. The middle classes were considered as benefiting from New Right public service reform, while those in the working class and growing underclass were not (Winlow and Hall, 2013).

Nevertheless New Labour continued with the same dedication to the now well established market-oriented education (Power and Whitty, 1999), which led to further disconnections between schools and local democratic processes. In their first years of power they continued to maintain many policy strands of the New Right. In parallel with this continued dedication to the market in schooling, New Labour were also in consideration of how competition did not seem to be working for disadvantaged communities. Somehow the educational market needed a compensatory intervention to better serve disadvantaged children. The adoption of a Third Way philosophy (Giddens, 1998) proved to be a mix of the market combined with public interventionism perhaps best described by Blair as the development of the notion of 'what works' (BBC, 2014). On one hand this philosophical stance nurtures a platform through which the market, such as that established in schooling in 1988, could be maintained, but it also allowed central government to intervene in the market where it was perceived not to be working. Overwhelming consumerism was now central to English schooling and this had served to weaken schools' relationships with their community and local democracy itself. Schools were viewed by parents as a consumerist choice; it was no longer considered the norm for the local school to be the natural choice for their children's education (Chamberlain *et al.*, 2006).

During the late 1990s a series of interesting experiments developed as New Labour attempted to learn how to adjust the market so those less advantaged families were not left behind. As had been the case since the introduction of the pseudo-market in schooling, disadvantaged children seemingly lost out in an education system that had become increasingly exploited to benefit the middle classes (Fielding and Moss, 2011).

In disadvantaged communities ideas similar to Plowden's recommendations (CACE, 1967) were rekindled and tested out by New Labour. Education Action Zones (EAZs) were piloted around the country in an attempt to 'join-up' services working with families, to see how this would improve educational results for disadvantaged children (Whitty, 2002). Sure Start Local Programmes (DfEE, 1998) were established in poorer communities with the aim of improving preschool learning and to tackle what throughout the New Labour years was identified as the fundamental problem of 'poor parenting' (Eisenstadt, 2011). This issue of the quality of parenting was considered central to the issue of intergenerational disadvantage (Field, 2011).

But, despite these moves, Blair was criticized for not doing enough to alleviate families labelled as socially excluded. Following research, a further major strand of policy emerged in the 'National Strategy for Neighbourhood Renewal 1999' (Cummings *et al.*, 2011). The interrelated nature of the issues that acted to place families at risk of social exclusion and the types of responses that could tackle these complex issues were high on Blair's agenda, epitomized by the establishment of the Social Exclusion Unit (SEU, 1998). This unit was wholly accountable to the Prime Minister's office. Policy Action Teams were established as a result of insights into the complex nature of issues families faced. Government-sponsored research reinforced how interrelated factors impacted upon families and that simplistic solutions such as improving teaching standards in schools would not turn around deep-seated intergenerational issues involving low attainment (SEU, 2001).

Following the launch of New Labour's manifesto (Labour Party, 1997) schools were viewed as key agents of social mobility and this conceptualization led to development of the Schools Plus policy (DfEE, 1999). This set out to review the role of schools in poor communities and how they could become agents to support community regeneration ambitions. The document proposed a vision for schools as centres of excellence for community involvement, and outlined a set of services that schools would be encouraged to adopt. These services included study support, adult learning and supporting young people to better connect with their community (DfEE, 1999). Cummings *et al.* (2011) claims this report set out the beginning of a sustained attempt to explore a new role for schools in the context of the new millennium. New Labour was experimenting with schooling and policy that might result in addressing their social justice ambitions.

The Full Service Extended School pilot activity followed in 2002/3 and proved to be one of many ways that New Labour tested the principles inherent in Schools Plus. LAs were asked to identify one school in their area sited in a disadvantaged community to which a grant could be awarded through which to test out a new role. In return LAs were expected to draw together a selection of local resources that could sustain the activity of the Full Service Extended School pilot once the grant had expired (Cummings *et al.*, 2006). These pilots were expected to develop a range of services reflecting the Schools Plus report, but these services were based upon local community needs assessments as opposed to a menu prescribed by central or local government.

The Every Child Matters agenda (DfES, 2003) arose out of policy thinking that became labelled as 'progressive universalism' (Cummings *et al.*, 2011). Research interviews with national policy makers and former Children's Ministers revealed how the Children and Young People's Unit of the Cabinet Office were responding to New Labour's social justice agenda and the findings from the Lord Laming Report into the death of Victoria Climbie. Every Child Matters promised a whole system reform of children and young people's services (Barker, 2009). It sought to bring together services that were seen as largely working 'in silos' and aimed to produce 'joined-up thinking' and 'joined-up working', which became phrases frequently used by Blair (2010). New Labour, like the previous successive Conservative governments was cautious about LAs; there was a shared distrust. Despite this cautiousness the Every Child Matters policy saw a revitalization of the role of LAs in children's lives (Martin, 2014). New powers were given to LAs to start a process of integrating children's services through the forming of Children's Trusts (UK Parliament, 2004). This included closer working with agencies such as the NHS and police but at this stage schools were not mandated to renew their relationship with LAs.

Experimenting with expanding the remit of all state funded schools commenced prior to any meaningful evaluation of the above piloting as DfES (2005) announced the prospectus 'Extended Schools: access to opportunities and services for all'. This asked every school to develop a Core Offer comprising out of [school] hours services for children, childcare provision, parenting support, family learning including access to adult education provision, and swift and easy referral of children to more specialist or targeted services. Like the Full Service Extended School pilots, schools had the freedom to design this offer to meet the needs of their community.

Interestingly Government and in turn LAs started a new dialogue with schools, which in some respects appeared rather contradictory. Schools remained in competition locally for pupils, and largely detached from LA influence, but were simultaneously asked to refresh their relationship with their LA, to deliver the new agenda of Every Child Matters, after many years of increasingly working with autonomy resulting from the 1988 Education Reform Act. Further to this it was to be delivered in most communities in England by clustering competing schools together and creating new relationships with LA funded services and wider community-based services sited within these clusters (DfES, 2005).

Whilst Full Service Extended Schools activity focused upon the most disadvantaged communities, Extended Schools, like the Every Child Matters policy (DfES, 2003) was about universalism together with a call for services based upon need (Campbell and Martin, 2011). *Extended Schools: Building on experience* (Department for Children, Schools and Families, 2007b) illustrates how schools had become viewed by New Labour's third term of government as pivotal organizations in the provision of local integrated children's and young people's services. Schools could provide a universal education offer, as they always had done, but this could be supplemented by facilitating additional, more targeted services, based upon individual children's need. The Government seemed set to attempt to achieve the Every Child Matters agenda via a more localized focus than LAs could offer (Carpenter *et al.*, 2012). The local partnerships that central government asked schools to form, coupled with community-based services provided a new localized platform for integrated service delivery which Mongon and Leadbeater (2012: 38) describe as placing 'schools located at the heart of the community' and led by the promotion of new school leadership roles or local 'system leaders' as Hargreaves (2010) described these.

New Labour's progressive policy development had a great influence upon school leaders and their workforce. Schools were autonomous bodies, well versed in competing with each other in a pseudo-market with parents choosing places for their children in successful schools (Power and Whitty, 1999). These school leaders had crafted internalized technical responses to improve school performance, which was their preoccupation when New Labour asked them to create new partnerships with other local schools (DfES, 2005), which were in most cases their competitors. School leaders and their workforce were then asked to look outside their school gates into the community to develop these partnerships to be inclusive of community-based services sited within the schools' host community and to start to engage in assessing the broader needs of children, young people and families (Broadhead and Martin, 2009). This challenge to school leaders intensified as DfES changed to become the Department of Children, Schools and Families (DCSF) followed by the publication of the *Children's Plan: Building a brighter future* (DCSF, 2007a).

The Children's Plan articulated New Labour's ambitions 'to make England the best place in the world for children and young people to grow up' (DCSF, 2007a: 3). It aimed to help parents and families support all children to succeed; for children and young people to enjoy childhood; to design services around the needs of children and families – not around professional boundaries; and to prevent failure rather than tackle crisis later.

Schools were now positioned not just to provide an Extended Schools Core Offer by 2010, but this plan set them the ambitious mission of becoming twenty-first-century schools at the heart of their community and to act as hubs for local comprehensive service delivery. The twenty-first-century school system involved excellent teaching; schools to identify and help address additional needs; providing a range of activities and opportunities to enrich the lives of children, families, and the wider community; and working more extensively and effectively with parents, other providers, and wider children's services (DCSF, 2008).

A former Children's Minister, from my research, suggested the Children's Plan and the twenty-first-century school represented a significant shift in rebalancing DCSF. The department had been dominated by schooling and the associated performance agenda and these new policy iterations represented a shift in departmental thinking towards more holistic engagement with childhood. The implication of this shift for English schooling encompassed the market in education and how schools were to become the key delivery mechanism for the Children's Plan shaped around localized, holistic, community needs. The former Children's Minister clarified the intention to implement the Every Child Matters agenda through schools as this seemed more achievable at a local level than it was proving to be at LA level. The twenty-first-century school marked a radical shift towards a new sense of localism as schools increasingly became viewed as a suitable vehicle to deliver service provision that could match community's needs and aspirations.

Carpenter *et al.* (2012) suggest that two-thirds of English schools were offering all five elements of the Core Offer as New Labour left power, with the remaining third providing some elements. Additionally the vast majority of schools had achieved this Core Offer via forming local partnerships of schools.

At the Extended Schools National Conference held in London in 2010 (DCSF, 2010), which in hindsight has been viewed as the twilight days of New Labour's regime, senior civil servants hailed the dawning of the new era for English schools. The Extended Schools Core Offer had been achieved within the schedule and schools were set to develop this role further through achieving the status of twenty-first-century schools.

Through the New Labour years, when the first half of this research was being conducted, schools and their leadership and workforce were shifting from education in its narrower sense to gain new understanding of what was involved in developing a broader approach to education.

Schooling 2010–2014

New Labour's experimenting with schools was brought to an abrupt end as the Coalition entered office in May 2010. Michael Gove, the new Secretary of State for Education, signalled a radical shift in policy by announcing a return to so-called 'traditional educational values' (Martin, 2014). The DCSF immediately became renamed the Department for Education (DfE) as it had been previously known under the New Right in the 1980s. This renaming of the department was also accompanied with a return to a focus on school governance, marketization, and a reduced role for LAs. Government websites were labelled with large disclaimers pronouncing policies held on them may not reflect the views and policy direction of the Coalition. Every Child Matters, Labour's flagship policy, and Extended Schools, through which it sought to deliver localized services, were at best ignored and at worst treated with contempt by the incoming Coalition (Martin, 2012).

The return to 'traditional educational values' meant further reform, perhaps more accurately described as a return to schooling solely focused upon the classroom and the quality of teaching delivered within this setting (Gove, 2010; Wilshaw, 2012). New Labour reforms were being disregarded (Facer, 2011) and replaced by a revitalized neoliberal, and neoconservative coalescence of the New Right (Ball, 2013). Coupled with this apparent reworking of 1980s policy was the conceptualization of Britain as broken (Cameron, 2009). The riots of August 2011 provided the Coalition with permission to build upon the construct of the undeserving underclass, confirming Britain was indeed broken and that the poor were feckless; a key theme of neoconservative thinking. Educational measures such as Troops for Teachers (HM Government, 2010) were what poor children needed, to be taught respect, and for schools to become centres for the control of unruly communities (Martin, 2014). Schools were set on a new course.

The decade of New Labour's progressive universalism, which provided school leaders and their workforce with permission to consider children in the much broader context of the family and community, was over. A return to the technical processes of classroom teaching and pupil control were back on the agenda and further to this schools were cutting their historic links with LAs and perhaps the partners they had recently discovered working with their pupils in the same community. The academy programme encouraged high-performing schools to convert to this new status. Although the Coalition attributed this programme to Blair's heritage, it was a sleight of hand. Blair had converted 'failing schools' to academies as opposed to the Coalition's fervour to convert 'outstanding schools', in effect to fracture school and LA relationships. In addition to the academy programme, a new stream of schooling, named free schools, was announced (Martin, 2014). These schools were to be established by parents in areas up and down the country and, like academies, they were to be directly funded by central government. This shift to extend school autonomy, while further centralizing the control of education, also served to fracture the links New Labour policy had tried to construct; a marked shift from community to consumerism. Chitty (2011) suggests that successful applications to set up free schools included a significant number focused upon specific interest groups, as opposed to the central concept of local parents coming together.

New Labour had attempted to bring together schools with community-based services through the Every Child Matters and Extended

Schools policies to support children and families in overcoming what Government considered to be barriers to achieving positive outcomes. The Coalition policy seemed intent on fragmenting service provision and separating schools, to focus purely upon so-called traditional education (Martin and Dunhill, 2013).

To further add to dilemmas in which the schools and the children and young people's workforce found themselves, through these shifting policy approaches, were also the reductions in public funding that increased throughout the Coalition's years in office. While schools and the NHS were only marginally affected by these, the funding for other services working with children and families was reduced. Examples include closure of Children's Centres, public libraries and the halving of youth service budgets (BBC, 2014). The Local Government Association (LGA, 2014) estimated some local authorities' budgets by 2015 had reduced by up to 40 per cent compared with their 2010 level.

International approaches to schooling: Perhaps there are some alternatives?

An early policy document produced by the Coalition, 'The Importance of Teaching' (DfE, 2010), described English schooling as falling down international league tables, in particular OECD PISA statistics concerning measures such as SATs results, as was the economy and competitiveness of the country. The globalization agenda fuelled the education reform debate discussed in the last section. New Labour imagined schools as an integral part of the community through which standards would be raised, particularly for those living in disadvantaged communities. But, the Coalition sought to find international solutions to the English schooling problem in relation to global challenges and chose two examples – one from the USA, the second from Sweden, through which to improve the country's international standing. The following sections will review these two international exemplars adopted by the Coalition, and also examine other models of schooling available in these two countries.

The USA and Full Service Schools

In the 1980s the New Right triumphed in both the UK and the USA in terms of the economy and restructuring public services, in particular in the context of schooling (Apple, 2001). It was to the USA that Coalition officials first looked for improved models of schooling. Michael Gove was particularly inspired by schooling in the USA based upon a coalescence of neoliberal and neoconservative approaches.

No Child Left Behind (USDoE, 2001) was implemented in response to the continued poor performance of children from disadvantaged communities across the USA. Central to this new agenda for schooling were solutions based upon accountability, choice, and flexibility in state-funded education. Increasing central accountability for schooling involved the introduction of challenging standards with annual testing across grades. Targets were associated with these schools tests and were published school by school and included the following aspects including race, ethnicity, poverty, disability, and English language proficiency, so that parents can make choices. Schools must meet the targets set for them to continue to gain state funding. Should schools fail to improve over a five year period with additional state funded support, the consequence would be a change of leadership, staff, and governance arrangements. Most commonly these schools have been converted to Charter Schools. This school structure involves the private sector, so more often than not a failing school would shift from being a public body to become a privately run organization.

However, despite No Child Left Behind, research suggests that this school system continues to suffer from similar issues associated with poorer children in England. Educators in the USA, like New Labour, had been searching for alternative models to those within the quasi-market and how to re-adjust the market in terms of a social justice agenda. As with English schooling, No Child Left Behind placed great emphasis upon internalized technically-based school improvement processes heavily linked to school marketization. But there are schools in the USA that engage with much broader understanding of children and families, going far beyond the confines of classroom teaching.

The Full Service School movement aims to address the issue of low levels of educational achievement and its link with poverty and disadvantaged communities. The concept behind the most prevalent model may well have inspired New Labour's experimentation between 2000 and 2010. Dryfoos (1998) discusses how during the 1990s Full Service Schools were developed in the USA in response to the situation in areas of high disadvantage and how children were not benefiting from the state schooling system as readily as their counterparts in wealthier communities. Further research demonstrates that there is a relatively long tradition in the USA of schools working closely with their communities with the aim to improve outcomes for children and to increase community aspirations. The Coalition for Community Schools (2014) has worked for many years to help Full Service Schools in becoming more community focused. It does this by supporting schools to operate in partnership with voluntary and statutory services based in their community. Through this, pupil learning is enhanced: by engagement with before and after school provision, through fun activities and also learning opportunities that help children better understand their community and how they may positively contribute towards it. Essential ingredients found within these schools or within their locality are services designed around the community, such as childcare, employment advice and training, housing and welfare benefits advice, and a range of health services (Cummings *et al.*, 2011).

According to Dryfoos (2002) the Full Service School recognizes, as does the Coalition for Community Schools, the complexity of issues that lead children to be less successful in educational terms when compared with their more affluent counterparts. Full Service Schools are based upon: 'strong partnership ideals and through these engage with broader service providers to fulfil their community's needs. This approach frees [school] teachers to teach by integrating critical child and family services into the fundamental design of the school' (Eisenhower Foundation, 2005: 6).

By constructing this response these schools are able to strengthen relationships with pupils, their changing needs and those of their family. The Chicago Federation for Community Schools supports 115 state-funded schools with over 15,000 pupils (Varlas, 2008). These schools provide an example of how a city and its communities have been subject to economic restructuring, similar to that of the communities that took part in this research study, and how they responded through their schools to fully engage with the challenges communities faced. Chicago schools hold central the common goals of helping pupils learn and strengthening families and through this improving their community.

Whalen (2007) outlines the strategies involved in order that schools may successfully engage with this important role. Each school is open through an extended day and this is managed by a resource co-ordinator; while the partnership to support this extended school venture engages school staff, parents, local religious organizations, local business people, and community-based organizations, jointly working to improve pupil outcomes. Through this approach Chicago's schools better understand and support the aspirations of families and their community. Whalen's research further suggests these schools compare favourably in academic terms with the performance of similar sized but less community-orientated schools. However, it was also noted that the communities where these community-based schools operate are subject to much higher levels of challenge such as poverty when compared to the communities of non-extended schools. A secondary finding of the research concerns school discipline: there were far lower levels of disciplinary referrals in the community–orientated/extended schools in Chicago.

The Harlem Children's Zone provides a more specific example of schooling in the USA that engages children in a much broader way. This initiative harnesses not merely local schools but a range of agencies that work in this disadvantaged area of New York (Cummings *et al.*, 2011). One could argue that this is not a purely school-based or school-led initiative when compared with the Dryfoos (2002) conceptualization of Full Service Schooling. However, closer examination demonstrates that the central feature of the work is a supportive 'pipeline' from 'cradle to career' and that indeed education is the central pillar of this community enterprise.

The Children's Zone was established in the 1990s as a project on one city-block (New York neighbourhood) and has steadily grown to now cover 97 blocks engaging with 12,300 children and 12,400 adults (HCZ, 2014). These blocks cover communities with high levels of deprivation and involve schools, community-based organizations, residents and stakeholders, to create a positive environment in which children can thrive. From early childhood, including parents and parenting support through the 'Baby College', elementary school, middle school and high school, the Children's Zones construct a pipeline of support through engagement with various services (Save the Children, 2012). Community-based services include health, housing, financial advice and support, and community centres, and through this joint activity creates programmes that strengthen and stabilize the community. The President of the USA, Barrack Obama, provides support for this project and, due to its success in assisting children to reach their aspirations, he has called for a network of such local partnerships to be replicated in other communities facing similar challenges to Harlem.

Save the Children, in their document *Developing Children's Zones: What's the evidence?* (2013), have started to construct versions of this Children's Zone model for communities in England. The rationale behind the introduction of such zones to disadvantaged communities in England is one that echoes with New Labour's experimentation in schooling, noted earlier. The continued level of poor outcomes associated with disadvantaged communities in England has led Save the Children to focus upon 'protective factors'. These factors have been identified with the aim of reducing the risk of the children's outcomes becoming negatively influenced and include issues such as poverty or low family aspiration. State funded schools are central to the Children's Zones proposed in England alongside neighbourhood services, drawing a remarkable resemblance to the Schools Plus report of 1999. And, in terms of educational achievement, 'children's zones aim to be holistic, intervening across all aspects of children's ecologies rather than focusing upon isolated issues or problems [such as educational attainment]' (Save the Children, 2013: 4).

The Coalition chose to refresh and drive forward once again an agenda of English schools in competition with each other citing the USA as an example of how to improve the country's position in global performance tables. This involved increased central government control and further detachment of schools from local democracy – and for that matter the communities in which they exist. However, in the USA the strong links between poverty and educational achievement remains and there are examples of more community-based models working to bridge this gap. Some of these models reflect principles of Extended Schools that the Coalition decided to ignore.

As English schooling narrowed, Swedish schooling broadened their understanding of what schools are

The Coalition's education advisors while investigating potential solutions to the English schooling 'problem' came across free schools in Sweden. In this model of schooling, Sweden's central government funded new schools proposed by parents or other groups, instead of the majority model where schools are funded and provided by local authorities. Today in Sweden there are nearly 800 of these publicly-funded private schools. Having visited Sweden in 2008, the future Conservative Education Secretary, Michael Gove, waxed lyrical:

> If we had Swedish-style reforms there is every reason to believe that we would have up to 3,000 new schools, all of them high quality and with an independent ethos ... The example of Sweden shows that it is not a distant utopia, it is a deliverable reform.
> (*The Guardian*, 2015)

Such ideological enthusiasm can blind politicians to the wider picture. Free schools in Sweden represent less than 10 per cent of children schooled in Sweden, though nearly 20 per cent of adolescents (Johansson and Moss, 2010). There are also signs that the movement is faltering: because of uncertainty about the future. Many Swedish free schools are run by companies for profit, analysis by Wiborg (2010) showing how, though parents have established free schools, private providers have taken them over. The result is that: 'Sweden has led the world in encouraging businesses to establish schools and remains the only country with a nationwide network of for-profit providers' (*TES*, 24 October, 2014). But with calls from the left to abolish such profit-making from education, Weale in *The Guardian* (10 June 2015) states 'fewer companies are coming forward to open new schools, banks are afraid to provide loans, and the numbers being approved to set up schools is going down'. Moreover, the results from this initiative have not been uniformly successful: Bergstrom and Wahlstrom (2008) identified a significant shift in secondary free schools from that of all-round education including citizenship towards a more mechanistic approach to prepare young people for work. And a further study into the impact of free schools on pupil achievement concluded there was no significant improvement when compared to the wider sector of Swedish schooling and in some cases there had been negative impacts (Wiborg, 2010).

But the attention given to the Swedish free school experiment has not been matched by that given to another and much more ambitious experiment: the development of the Swedish 'extended school'. Following the decentralization of schooling from central to local government in the early 1990s, which already had responsibility for early childhood education and 'free time' services (for children to attend outside school hours), schools have developed to include 'pre-school classes' (for 6 year olds, previously in early childhood centres) and free-time services. They have become services for 6 to 16 year olds, open throughout the day, often from 7 a.m. to 6 p.m. In some cases, early childhood centres have been linked to schools, so that the school rektor (headteacher) has overall responsibility for children from one year of age through to 16 years.

But this has not been achieved by simply tacking-on 'nursery classes' and 'out-of-school care' to a core school, 'wraparound care' in the thoughtless jargon of English policy. Instead, an ambitious attempt has been made to reconfigure the school based on multi-professional teams involving three graduate professions – early childhood teachers, school teachers, and free-time pedagogues. The aim is that, while sharing values and goals, each profession will bring its own particular knowledge, skills, and perspectives to the team. Swedish schools today, at least for children under 11 years, are typically organized into mixed age groupings of children, each group with a multi-professional team of workers. In the groups for younger children, up to 10 or 11 years, this team will consist of pre-school teachers, school teachers, and free-time pedagogues. This staff group works with children across the school day; while school teachers, because of different working hours, are not generally with the group at the beginning and end of the day, pre-school teachers and free-time pedagogues work across the extended school day, including alongside school teachers during what are described as school hours. Unlike England, there is no separate 'wraparound' school-age childcare service, nor a separate, lower qualified group of school-age childcare workers (Johansson and Moss, 2010).

The importance attached to teamworking led originally to a radical reform of professional education, with all those wanting to work in pre-school or school first undertaking an 18-month common education, before deciding in which profession to specialize and subsequently taking more specialist modules. This has subsequently been modified, as early childhood and free-time work seemed to many to lose out, with most students choosing to go on to specialize in school teaching, with the other professions feeling at risk of losing numbers, standing, and identity. Today, therefore, students once again decide what course to follow before they enter university, though there remain some modules shared by all three professions.

Other problems have been reported, again often bound up with professional relationships. School teachers retain somewhat better employment conditions than either early childhood teachers or free-time pedagogues, typically not participating in work with children outside specified 'school hours' (and the continuing differentiation between 'school time' and other times shows again the limits of integration). A number of principles for successful teamworking have been identified: common goals; team members feeling confident that they are allowed to develop their own work and to test new ideas in their daily practice; team members recognizing that cooperation is the best way to undertake their respective tasks; cooperation proving rewarding for all team members; consensus about when and how cooperation should take place; cooperation being recognized as a condition for collective learning processes (Ohlsson, 2004). But identifying such principles and making them work in practice are two very different things. Genuine teamworking can be fraught, with hierarchies emerging, not least some school teachers asserting a leadership role, and treating their professional colleagues more in the role of assistants.

So behind the attention-grabbing attempts to set up a marketized and privatized education, the great majority of Sweden's schools, in the public sector and in close relationship with local authorities, have been struggling to create a broader school, one where care, education and leisure are closely intertwined, based on a broader idea of education and on developing new relationships between different professions with long traditions of working with children. While not as broad in concept as the English Extended School

– notably lacking the focus on families and community – Swedish schools have been attempting to develop a more holistic approach to children and education.

Swedish education is going through a period of crisis, at the time of writing, with plummeting rankings on PISA, increased inequality and controversy about the role of free schools in this decline. Perhaps one lesson to be drawn is the difficulty of adopting two policies, each pointing in different directions. Whether you believe in free schools or extended schools, they both need a lot of careful attention to implement. They represent very different policies and politics, and trying to pursue both at the same time may be a recipe for neither succeeding on its own terms.

Summary

This chapter has raised a range of issues that directly relate to both setting the context for this research and the insights and understandings generated by it. We have seen how English schooling has been embedded within local democracy and its processes for over 80 years. During this time it has gained a heritage that considered children in a much broader context than that constructed through the implementation of the 1988 Education Reform Act. The concept of schools positioned centrally within their community has a rich history, particularly in the context of disadvantaged communities, although this concept has been in and out of favour over the last hundred years. Schools being perceived as organizations that fail children from poorer communities is not a new phenomenon and is one that has preoccupied those concerned with education for many years. Solutions can be traced to the 1920s through the formalization of schools as central to their community.

The impact of the neoliberal and neoconservative inspired policy deeply impacted upon schools and educators and when New Labour started to experiment with their reforms, and the professionalism associated with them, they introduced potentially radical approaches to schooling. However, these short lived trials abruptly concluded in policy terms as the Coalition took office. Further centralization of education followed based upon a refreshed neoliberal agenda combined with a construct of traditional schooling based upon neoconservative philosophy. Though the Coalition borrowed these refreshed models of competition from countries such as the USA and the free school model from Sweden, in those same countries there are also alternatives to these approaches. Case-studies constructed from data produced by the research will provide insights into how four diverse partnerships of schools responded to New Labour's experimentation with schooling and what happened when the Coalition of 2010 sought to change the direction of schooling.

Chapter 2

Orpintown: Extended Schools and a market town

Introduction

Each of the following four chapters will focus upon a case-study constructed through the analysis of data collected between 2006 and 2014, generated by this longitudinal research. Each case-study provides a unique insight into the impact of challenging policy development upon differing communities and the understandings that emerged are central to this book. Responses played out in differing ways in each community, with the key tension being between education in its broader and narrower conceptualizations. A timeline, which provides a guide to central government policy development in relation to Extended School, can be found in Appendix 1, while the key milestones for each partnership are listed in Appendix 2.

This chapter is concerned with Orpintown, which can be broadly described as a market town. Chapter 3 will engage with developments in Gadley, a former coalmining community. Both of these communities are sited within Eastfield LA. A brief description of Orpintown and its schools will set the background to this case-study and will be followed by an account of the development of Extended Schools. This was a complex and lengthy journey for all concerned requiring a highly skilled leader to appreciate the differing interests and understanding of community-based services who might become future local partners. In 2007 schools were working in isolation from each other, with a clear divide between primary and secondary education. Community-based organizations were working in a similar way, with little knowledge of each other or of their contributions to the lives of children and families. There were deep-rooted tensions in moving towards broader approaches to children and families, which took many years to overcome. By 2011 a strong partnership had grown but this was challenged by new Coalition policy development. But despite this new policy direction the partnership continued to progress its new found understandings of children and families.

Orpintown: the community and schools

Orpintown is a market town that local residents considered had retained its community identity despite being absorbed into a large LA approximately 35 years ago. They also perceived Eastfield LA as largely preoccupied by the issues of its city and in particular the social problems of its inner city communities. Orpintown is situated 20 miles from Eastfield city and is separated by 'green-belt' farmland. Conversations with local residents revealed pride in the Town Council, which still provided a range of services such as funding voluntary sector organizations and events despite local government reorganization some 40 years ago that significantly marginalized its powers. In 1974 the newly formed Eastfield LA took over all statutory functions from the town and county councils. Orpintown Town Council was still able to raise local taxes but did not play a role in key areas of public services such as schooling, planning, or refuse disposal, for example.

Headteachers and area managers discussed how the majority of children and young people's service provision was managed from the distant city centre council offices of Eastfield LA and the NHS Primary Care Trust (PCT) as it was then known. PCTs were administrative bodies responsible for the commissioning of health services in England between 2001 and 2013.

A resident, during a conversation in a local community centre, reflected upon the relevance of the schools' role in the context of Orpintown community set against a host of key services managed from the distant administrative centre:

> What is this school [the local primary school] for? We used to have a local community where we all belonged [including broader services] which had values shared by the community. You may have had a quarrel or a punch up but these were checked by the community … It is false [the management services through Eastfield] … and it is very difficult as now there are no local shared community principles or values.

A brief profile of Orpintown

Orpintown has a broad spectrum of family-based services such as Children's Social Care and the Youth Service sited within the town centre, but there were concerns about a lack of local specialist services to provide support to families with additional or complex needs, an example being young people's mental health provision. Despite its semi-rural location, public transport links were viewed as good between the town and local cities and across village communities. Statistics provided by the LA revealed that many people commuted daily to work in Eastfield city or the second nearby city of Westfield. Unlike nearby cities, there were no significant numbers of Black, Asian and Minority Ethnic communities in the town or families from mainland Europe. A local councillor stated the population was 'stable when compared with that of Eastfield city'. Unemployment across Orpintown was low and those unemployed were largely people moving between jobs.

There was one social housing estate in the town, Redbury, with higher than national average unemployment and high poverty. Detailed localized profiles provided by the LA described the socio-economic make-up of the villages around Orpintown where most of its primary schools were located. These were affluent communities with marginal unemployment and a majority of housing was owner-occupied. The town retained elements of its heritage reflected through local music, arts, sport, and farming events. Its rural setting and agricultural heritage were important considerations for the community although the reality was Orpintown had become a commuter area.

The schools in Orpintown and its surrounding villages

Orpintown high school is close to the town centre and catered for over 1,400 pupils. It drew young people from the town and villages and, due to its positive image as a 'good school', from neighbouring LAs as it bordered three LAs. Orpintown high school was inspected by Ofsted in 2013 and the outcome reflected the earlier inspections of 2004 and 2007 being across the spectrum of 'good' to 'outstanding'. The principal said the high school 'is in the top 25 per cent of schools in the country in relation to achievement at A level and a high proportion of students move onto university'. The principal resigned his post during the early period of the field research to take up a new role of managing a number of 'failing schools' in the LA. An acting principal led the high school throughout the main period of the research and was followed by a new permanent appointment. The latter converted the school into an academy, under the Coalition's first round in 2011, enabled by its high-performing status.

Eight primary schools were also part of Orpintown's developing partnership. Each school was managed by a headteacher and governing body with support from the LA. Despite its geographical remoteness from the administrative centre of Eastfield, conversations with headteachers revealed 'the schools had retained strong relationships with the LA'. Throughout the field research, headteachers were considering other governance options; however, the high school was the only one to convert to academy status.

The eight primary schools in the partnership, other than Redbury, had similar 'good' or 'outstanding' assessments by Ofsted. Redbury Primary School, which serves an estate with high deprivation, was considered to be 'a good school' by residents but 'adequate' by Ofsted at its last two inspections. Orpintown's schools' Ofsted reports noted their popularity and high subscription rates, which headteachers were very proud of, and added to the sense of a confident community with a strong local identity.

The high school had hosted an adult education programme open to the community, predating the concept of Extended Schools by some ten years. Although wholly run and managed by the high school, and being one of the elements of government's requirement for the Core Offer, it did not seem to be viewed by the school as part of this offer. The high school also provided local residents with extensive sports facilities, which again were not considered to contribute to the Core Offer. 'A new and more welcoming' reception block was built in 2006 to ease access to the high school and its facilities for local residents. But, the principal said: 'this was built using the high school's budget to respond to their growing role in relation to the community'. The existing adult education provision and sports centre signified the organizational dominance of this school in the town. But these were viewed locally as part of an historic legacy, accidentally sited in the school rather than contemporary in nature and linked to the Extended Schools agenda.

Moving towards Extended Schools

The research commenced in Orpintown in 2007, which marked what was known locally as 'phase two' of Extended Schools. This followed the appointment of the first Extended Schools manager, which was viewed as 'unsuccessful' by headteachers, a second phase commenced and was marked with the secondment of a senior manager from the high school as outlined in the timeline found in Appendix 2.

Eastfield LA promoting Extended Schools development

The Extended Schools agenda was initially introduced to Orpintown by Eastfield LA, which also provided funding for the informal local partnership that had survived since the early 1990s. These partnerships represented attempts by the LA to encourage schools to work together locally. However, the pressure of competition meant that these partnerships were of little significance despite Orpintown's schools (and Gadley's schools featured in the next chapter) receiving a small fund provided by the LA. The LA had also channelled other funds, such as New Labour's Excellence in Cities initiative (DfEE, 1999), through these informal partnerships, but despite this local school leaders considered partnership working of low priority.

The high school leadership readily took ownership of the new Extended Schools agenda on behalf of Orpintown community and considered it 'a natural progression of my leadership role'. The principal described how he 'chaired the meeting and as such led many developments in the area' and the 'Extended Schools Board was established to coordinate effective deployment of services in the area and encourage partnership working'.

The principal also alluded to a first abortive attempt to bring the primary schools into a formalized Extended Schools partnership. A new member of staff had been employed by the high school as Extended Schools Manager; however, a second attempt was necessary through seconding a highly experienced senior manager who was the high school's lead on pupils with Special Educational Needs (SEN). The first attempt's failure was attributed to the lack of status and credibility of the appointee in the eyes of primary school headteachers, whilst the second appointment carried 'more gravitas'. But despite this appointment, ongoing discussions about why schools need to work in partnership continued to come from some primary school headteachers. Eastfield LA, in response to this continued poor interschool relationship and their failure to develop an Extended School partnership, increased pressure on Orpintown's schools to gain a more positive response. This second attempt at implementing Extended Schools, commencing in 2007, eventually led to the development of the partnership central to this research.

Who should lead Extended Schools?
Orpintown high school was a much larger organization than the individual local primary schools clustered around its catchment area. The high school's staffing structure and its budget equalled that of half the primary schools in the partnership. Arguably its management was also 'far more complex than that of primaries' with their single form intakes. Despite this differentiation, the leaders of the primary schools collectively considered themselves better equipped to develop the Extended Schools agenda than the high school. This proved to be an ongoing issue in relation to the development and management of Extended Schools. A primary school headteacher insisted 'Every Child Matters is the way primary schools work, meeting the needs of children and their families. We have different priorities to those leading secondary education!' Primary sector leaders considered the management of Extended Schools was more naturally their territory as the policy was viewed as closely

related to the Every Child Matters policy agenda and they considered they exhibited a greater degree of community orientation compared to Orpintown high school. Another primary school headteacher reflected a consensus held across the sector that 'our role is to educate children in the widest possible sense', as opposed to the high school, which was considered as 'narrower in its education and driven by examination results'.

LA staff discussed how they attempted to bring local schools together using, for example, an Excellence in Cities funding stream to ask schools to consider more mutual work during this first phase of developing Extended Schools. Excellence in Cities was a government approach set up in urban schools, which sought to diversify school provision by engaging with broader understandings of children than those of pupils in the classroom so all of their needs could be met. This approach was particularly focused upon Key Stage 3 pupils in relation to attainment. In Orpintown this type of funding eventually led to the Learning Support Unit (LSU) facility, which opened as the research commenced.

The second and much more successful appointment of the high school's SEN coordinator to become Extended Schools Manager helped ease this divide in primary and secondary schooling, as the new educator brought with her a deep knowledge and broad understanding of the support services required to assist pupils with SEN. This included some knowledge of the primary sector, but more particularly support for SEN pupils and their families in the transition to secondary education. But first there was a need to bring the schools together. The Extended Schools Manager described how 'Extended Schools is having a significant effect upon my daily work. I can say it is every day I work on this. I am in and out of schools a great deal, in the community communicating with people and I am currently feeling very positive about the journey.'

However a primary school headteacher continually alluded to the ongoing friction between Orpintown's schooling sectors, 'friction, you [the researcher] may pick up on in meetings between the primary and secondary school leaders', and provided a hint as to a further issue, 'more power needs to be devolved by the chair'. But it also appeared the primary sector was not united over Extended Schools development.

Building trust between headteachers

With ongoing tensions between primary and secondary school leaders, a sense of mistrust between primary school leaders was also evident. Schools remained in competition with each other for pupil numbers and league table positions. However some primary school leaders discussed the differentiated approach taken to Every Child Matters, emerging through the newly devised Ofsted framework, leading to the 2006 Education and Inspection Act when schools were required to promote the well-being of their pupils. Some school leaders felt the framework reflected their views of the role of primary educators, whilst others considered it somehow shifted the teaching profession from their primary role of teaching to take on a role of carer and removed responsibilities from parents. It appeared some leaders remained focused upon narrow performativity measures while others were engaging with the pressure for schools to respond to the increasing demands of the Every Child Matters agenda. Similarly some primary headteachers attended the Board meetings while others appeared to ignore the broader agenda emerging through Extended Schools. One who supported it explained her vision: 'the new school will be open seven days per week and all year round, delivering a broad range of facilities', and 'the Every Child Matters agenda is now central to our school planning'. The Extended Schools Manager confirmed this differing stance 'initially some primary schools found it difficult to engage because they did not understand the Core Offer'. Despite the historical roots of the informal partnership, the joint development of the Learning Support Unit (LSU) in 2008 and a shared pride in the town, it appeared that the schools knew little about each other nor was there a sense of collective ownership among the schools of their common role as local educators.

Schools and their remoteness from their community

The Extended Schools Manager, despite extensive experience in SEN and the links to multi-agency working entailed in her job, discussed how 'when I first took the job I had to find out who was who [in the community] and try to get them around the table to talk about Extended Schools'. This reflected the high school's remoteness from community-based services, and lack of knowledge about what they delivered and to whom. The second task was to use her considerable skills learnt in the SEN and Assistant Headteacher roles to engage with these services on behalf of the partnership, which at this stage consisted only of local schools.

In terms of the community and starting to understand it, the Extended Schools Manager used research on the Redbury estate. This local research was carried out by a church group with the aim to better understand local community needs. It resulted in the forming of the Redbury Residents' Association and the revitalization of the local community centre. The church-led research informed and acted as the first stage in developing Orpintown's Extended Schools needs analysis and led to the first engagement with community-based services including the Town Council.

Orpintown: Extended Schools and a market town

Town councillors participated in school governing bodies and also joined the new meetings that directly supported the development of the Extended Schools 'Core Offer'. Part of the funding for this development work was provided by the town council from local taxes and was additional to Eastfield LA's funding. The town councillors could see how this emerging partnership might provide a new local platform with which they could work and that would enable them to play a part in service provision that was traditionally the domain of the LA. Voluntary sector agencies had evolved locally and participants commented upon how these had become part of the everyday life of the town, but seemingly not of the schools.

Further engagement by the Extended School Manager secured contributions of the Youth Service, police, faith groups [linked with the aforementioned research], local sports charities, health professionals, and Children's Social Care. These contributions included funding, staff time, and commitment and served to bring this diversity of organizations together to start to discuss new ways of delivering services locally. Engaging in conversations led to the question of establishing formal governance arrangements for Extended Schools working. Table 2.1 illustrates the governance arrangements of the Extended Schools Board and the services that engaged in the development and delivery of Orpintown's Extended Schools partnership. The Board consisted of schools as voting members plus non-school services who also attended meetings but were not empowered to vote. The subgroups that also formed to support these new partnership developments can be viewed in Tables 2.2 and 2.3. These subgroups were the places where plans were implemented with new services being tested out in response to the requirement to provide a Core Offer.

School-dominated governance arrangements

The governance arrangements developed proved to be rather school dominated and hierarchical in nature. The principal and partnership chair argued these arrangements were intended 'to coordinate the effective development of services in the area and encourage partnership working'. And, when asked why schools should seemingly dominate the partnership, the principal replied: 'we [schools] have long understood that some of our pupils need positive activities beyond the school day. This helps to ensure that they receive additional planned support and guidance when this can be lacking in the home environment.' And of his leadership role emerging through Extended Schools policy development he added that:

> ... the government is right in placing its trust in schools and the leadership of schools. We have for many years now produced

the outcomes to match targets laid down by government. We have delivered success. We are well aware we have been closely monitored [by successive governments] and we have put in place effective strategies to achieve our targets. This Extended Schools agenda adds to this.

Table 2.1 Orpintown governance arrangements

Orpintown's Extended Schools Board	Governance structure
Chair	High school principal
Servicing the Board	Orpintown's Extended Schools Manager based in high school
Voting members	Eight school governors primary sector
	Eight school headteachers primary sector
Non-voting members	Police
	LA Youth Manager
	LA Social Care Manager
	LA Early Years Manager
	NHS representative
	LA Extended Services Development Manager
Purpose	To form a local partnership, devise governance arrangements, and take responsibility for the strategic development of Extended Schools in the Orpintown area

Observations of the newly established Extended Schools Board demonstrated an approach that appeared to have little to do with partnership working. The schools' headteachers and governor representatives sat on the Board and awarded themselves voting rights; whilst those who were starting to enter into partnership working, such as Children's Social Care or NHS services, brought resources to the partnership but could not influence the Board's decision-making processes or its direction of travel. While the Extended School Manager used her considerable skills to engage with these services, there was noticeable dissent from key players on the subject of 'partnership versus takeover'. The Youth Work Manager was concerned that 'schools are very much interested in trying to develop services delivered by them instead of working in partnership to improve services'. And a Children's Social Care Manager described how after many years of poor communication with schools 'it feels like education is the big player. There are several representatives from differing schools and me sat there on my own. Sometimes it feels a bit overwhelming. It appears we are lesser players.'

But these organizations worked with local schools to construct new local services as they realized this was emerging as central government's preferred way of delivering services to children.

The business of developing new local services

The real development work to deliver Extended Schools was observed taking place in two subgroups of the Extended Schools Board summarized in Tables 2.2 and 2.3. One was concerned with developments of the Core Offer of services including summer programmes and before and after school activities. The second dealt with what were considered 'problem children'. This involved a wide range of practitioners coming together to discuss responses where schools identified children who were not succeeding educationally. This work complemented the new Common Assessment Framework (CAF) being implemented locally. The CAF was central to national government's agenda of bringing services together to address children's needs. Both of these groups promoted multi-professional working locally, but with different emphases.

Observations of these meetings revealed that schools knew little about each other or other local services; community-based services similarly knew little about each other. This lack of understanding extended to the core purpose of other organizations and the children they were working with. Seemingly this was the first time services had come together, despite often working with the same families in the same community. Like schools coming together to learn about each other, non-school services were also learning about each other. It was a local journey of discovery for all concerned, which also proved to be a long and protracted journey.

Broader learning was also taking place outside these meetings and throughout the differing workforces. A police officer observed that: 'in the past we have talked about multi-agency working approaches but it has not worked. People have not worked together' and now 'my role is to explain the criminal justice system to professionals like teachers. A lot of them are not aware of what we [the police] do with children.'

An Early Years Manager reflected upon the local leadership of schools and how they had little knowledge of what lay beyond the school gates. But added positively that 'I think there is huge potential for schools to be part of the community and integral to the community, but at present schools organize themselves more internally'.

In 2009 a local faith-worker summed up the mood of both schools and their newly discovered partners and what the Extended Schools Manager referred to as 'the progress they had made on a long journey that could take 10 years to deliver'. The worker commented that: 'it is quite interesting because I have been to that Extended Schools meeting for a while. Sat there, drank tea and eaten biscuits and now actions are attached to these meetings. It was let's do this and delegate that ... these meetings have really helped us develop. It is really positive now.'

Table 2.2 Orpintown Partnership Universal Services subgroup

Universal work with families subgroup	Accountable to the Extended Services Board
Key aims are through coherent local multi-agency planning to deliver	A varied menu of activities for children and families
	A range of study support opportunities
	Other activities as directed by the Extended Schools Board
Chair of the meeting	Orpintown's Extended Services Manager
Members included	Town councillors
	Town council staff
	Local sports charity representative
	Local church representatives
	Local arts charity representative
	National voluntary organization representative
	LA Youth Work representative
	LA Early Years representative

Table 2.3 Orpintown Partnership Targeted Family Services subgroup

Targeted Families Subgroup	Accountable to the Extended Services Board
Key aims: to work with families identified by school staff to develop localized working arrangements to improve children and young people's outcomes	Key areas engaged with: Swift and easy referral Support CAF developments Analyse CAF responses Facilitate effective local working
Chair of meeting	Orpintown's Extended Schools Manager
Members included	Headteachers or SENCOs or inclusion leaders or other school staff Children's Centre staff NHS staff Attendance officer Children's Social Care Manager Children's social workers Police Other staff dealing with family issues as appropriate
Outcome of this subgroup	This subgroup developed multi-professional approaches to respond to the needs of children and families that lived in the area. This multi-professional practice was new to Orpintown and prevented children falling into Children's Social Care interventions and provided a route out of social care.

Learning to understand each other's perspective and potential conflict

Over time the partnerships' subgroups grew in confidence as they 'tried out things', discussed outcomes of programmes, and overcame the sense of mistrust that was evident at the early stages of the research. The headteachers and partnership leaders, alongside this growing local bonding associated with the construction of new, more integrated service responses, started to question some of the services' responses being delivered at strategic LA level. A new tension developed between the strengthening local partnership and LA and NHS strategic staff dealing with services across the LA. One case concerned Eastfield LA's Children's Social Care Service. A Children's Social Care Manager divulged:

> I met two headteachers recently to talk through some issues. They had a bad experience with some of our people they went to meet ... they were senior managers from my department which concerns me. The headteachers felt really like they were not being respected ... and if at this level [Senior Social Care Managers] they are making schools feel alienated, we are going to have difficulties locally.

A headteacher who was also part of the Extended Schools developments was present at this meeting and commented on LA leaders' lack of commitment to partnership working in that 'we need Children's Social Care [senior managers] to engage with us! If Social Care is more engaged, we would improve things.'

A further tension arose from the plans and actions that were being generated. This was described by a local health worker, who was also a key player in both subgroups. She discussed how her NHS managers instructed her that Extended Schools was not part of her role in Orpintown: 'We have been instructed not to get heavily involved with Extended Schools. We are not actually commissioned to be involved. It is not actually recognized by PCT commissioners.'

Despite facing many similar problems, by 2011 localized partnership workings had become recognized by Eastfield LA and to some extent their arrangements were being formalized by the LA. However the outcomes of NHS reforms were not clear so the position of health services remained rather confused. Despite the hostility and tensions between schools and community-based services, the Extended Schools Manager constructed a productive local partnership that introduced a range of new services to Orpintown. A selection of these services are illustrated in Table 2.4 including health and sport programmes, preschool programmes for young children and their parents, and local community activities such as festivals. This long process of learning from each other to construct new practice was in full flow when the national government changed at the 2010 General Election.

Table 2.4 Orpintown Partnership: a selection of services developed

The services developed by Orpintown Extended Schools partnership included:
- The facilitation of localized integrated multi-professional working around families – a radical shift in emphasis from crisis intervention associated with Children's Social Care to one of early intervention and prevention; including support for step-down from Children's Social Care interventions into more universal services
- Range of health programmes for children in primary and secondary school, e.g. healthy eating courses
- Sports programmes for children in primary and secondary schools
- Preschool programmes involving parents and younger children
- Parenting programmes
- Involving parents in their child's education so that they better understood school processes
- Programmes to improve school timekeeping and attendance
- Community health activities such as community walks
- Community activities for all, including art, music, drama, play
- Local festival activities such as the agricultural festival, art, music, drama
- Before and after school activities, including breakfast clubs and homework clubs
- Extensive range of school holiday programmes for young children through to youth
- Family support programmes
- Children's Centre developments and understanding the range of local childcare provision
- Preschool transition programmes
- Transition programmes between primary and secondary education
- Financial advice in partnership with CAB
- Careers and job fairs to aid young people and parents access further training and job opportunities

The Coalition, academization, and Orpintown's partnership

The change in government signalled a new policy direction that started to impact upon Orpintown's Extended Schools partnership. In 2010 the Coalition disregarded much of New Labour policy including the Every Child Matters and Extended Services policies. But also in 2012 the high school moved to academy status under the Coalition's policy that claimed to 'free schools further from local bureaucracy'. The high school was judged by Ofsted as 'outstanding' and as such able to detach itself from its LA relationship despite strong opposition campaigns in the community. The outcry from the community was also supported by primary school headteachers, community leaders, and broader services that had engaged in the Extended Schools agenda.

The newly appointed Extended Schools Manager following the retirement of the previous manager discussed openly the issue of her employer, the Academy, in relation to Extended Schools: 'the academy stuff last term is an interesting one ... one thing we [the management of the academy] stressed during the local academy debate is that the partnership will not be put in danger'. And she went on to say, 'there is an issue about not being a LA school now. It is an issue of paperwork essentially. It has not caused any practicalities to change because the Extended Schools partnership is strong.'

All partners feared that this shift to academy status would cause the local partnership to collapse. However, a primary school leader in 2012 said 'I am really opposed to academies, but, I have not noticed any difference in how the high school has worked with us since converting compared to before'.

The headteacher moved on to discuss how the headteachers of local primary schools now engage in a dialogue of partnership and of their opposition to the Coalition's return to a refreshed market place in schooling 'we [Orpintown's schools] very much support each other for mutual benefit' and of interschool competition 'it is not now how we work'.

Over a seven year period Orpintown's partnership had grown from one riven with complex tensions to become a conduit through which Eastfield LA could deliver some of its children's services agenda.

An analysis of the Orpintown experience

This section will draw out some key themes that emerged from the research over the period 2007 to 2014.

Leading Extended Schools: Someone with status required

The role of Extended Schools Manager in this partnership proved to be one involving multiple and complex challenges. Though the high school and its feeder primaries had been engaged in an 'informal partnership for some years' and they were jointly working on developing a LSU, in 2007 there was little evidence of inter-school working or cross-school understanding in Orpintown. These schools, but not the high school, had been in competition with each other for almost two decades in terms of attracting pupils and league table positions. A highly skilled school leader 'with gravitas' was required to ensure schools began to engage with each other.

Orpintown's schools were very much on 'catch-up', in terms of the Extended Schools and Every Child Matters policies, when the research commenced in 2007. Their first attempt led by the high school failed and was attributed to the new member of staff having 'a lack of currency' with school leaders. The principal reacted by seconding a highly skilled and experienced school leader who through the SEN role understood aspects of multi-agency working. This Assistant Headteacher commanded the respect of primary school leaders, was a recognized member of a successful school leadership team and demonstrated a high level of interpersonal and professional skills.

Schools competition, cooperation, or both?

The Extended Schools Manager considered that bringing schools together was key in order that mutual working could commence, as schools were charged with leading local partnership working. It appeared school competition had overridden any sense of mutuality despite all schools subscribing to the concept of a local market-town heritage and pride. But not all primary headteachers engaged with the Extended Schools agenda. Tensions between these leadership figures continued to be aired as some positively contributed to new developments and others ignored it. In Extended Schools Board meetings some primary headteachers discussed the consistent absence of colleagues and in research interviews similar issues arose. Personal principles came to the fore in developing this local expression of Every Child Matters policy, with those enthusiastic about a wider agenda contributing and other leaders continuing with the more narrow school performativity agenda. Bringing schools together to build the partnership on mutual understanding was not an easy matter, even with a skilled and respected manager leading developments.

Differing professionalism: Primary and secondary education

There was also a deep divide, linked to a lack of understanding of basic practice and approaches, between primary and secondary educators. Despite a majority of pupils transitioning from these primary feeders to the high school there was little in the way of cross-sector cooperation at this vital transition. The divide expressed itself as a tension fuelled by the high school's view that they were the 'natural leader of Extended Schools' developments. Primary school leaders who attended development meetings considered themselves more engaged with parents and the broader community than the high school. The governance arrangements that were developed to support Extended Schools reflected the high school's dominance through ownership of the chair role, hosting, and servicing the meetings. The Extended Schools Manager used her considerable skills and expertise to develop positive relationships with the primary school leaders despite their differing views of the value of the local partnership and, over time headteachers and their staff started to form new understandings of each other, their roles and the rationale behind each school's priorities. By 2012 there seemed to be a strong bond developed between all the primary schools and the partnership, but this was to be severely challenged by the high school's shift to 'academy status'.

Schools needing to learn about their community

Turning towards the community, despite the Extended Schools Manager's experience of multi-agency working in the context of SEN, neither she nor the schools had any understanding or knowledge of the diversity of agencies working in the community. An inroad into this ignorance was the church-led research that provided insights into the most deprived community in the area. The Extended Schools Manager's priority was to 'go out into the community and get services around the table'. And, as these services progressively engaged they also realized they knew little about these inwardly looking schools.

These community-based services also realized they understood little of who also worked with children in the community besides themselves. This was regardless of the nature or purpose of the organizations, that is whether they were statutory or non-statutory, and how they worked with children or their families. Perhaps the only exception to this was Children's Social Care in the context of families in crises where services historically were required to come together and share information with the aim to protect children from serious harm. The Extended Services Board and the two subgroups established to progress local developments were the first occasions when these services had come together face to face within Orpintown.

Developing mutual understandings and missed opportunities to learn

Mutual learning took place within these new meeting structures about approaches, practice, and measures of success and these community-based services even discovered some organizations were working with the same children. School staff and community-based services started to pool their knowledge, skilfully facilitated by the Extended Schools Manager, to construct new multi-professional forms of practice. This practice was described as 'early intervention' and used the new tool, known as 'the CAF'. Observation of meetings demonstrated new understandings of families were emerging across these services including schools. Schools, which had previously dealt with individual children, were beginning to realize that siblings may be in other schools and that there were other services working with their pupils in the community. They also began to pool their knowledge, skills and experience to develop new local programmes such as 'before and after school clubs' and 'holiday activities'. Eventually by 2008 budgets began to be pooled but this caused some further issues of contention locally between these newfound partners, through missed opportunities to learn, particularly in terms of governance and leadership.

Orpintown high school as 'natural leaders' took a school-focused approach to developing governance arrangements. This was linked to a culture where 'schools had delivered targets for government', therefore assuming other services had somehow not delivered as successfully. This approach was primarily characterized by a deficit pathway based upon pupils who were considered by schools as being academically unsuccessful due to poor support at home. The governance arrangements provided schools with almost total control over the direction of Orpintown's Extended School programme. The arrangements asked and expected non-school based services such as the NHS or Children's Social Care to contribute but allowed them little, if any, leadership input into the local model. This represents a missed opportunity to learn from the leaders of community-based services. These community-based organizations resented this position as schools had only a partial interest and understanding of how these agencies worked and what were their measures of success. The Early Years, Youth Service, and Children's Social Care managers, while realizing how new ways of working could improve outcomes for their children and families, were also under pressure from Eastfield LA to work in prescribed ways. This issue was also the case with NHS staff as their service specifications were commissioned by the PCT with no regard for the emerging Extended Schools agenda. It appeared that local partnerships, while constructing new ways of working were also viewing children and families in a new way, but at a more strategic level in the LA and PCT managers continued to set targets and measure priorities within a framework based on long-established 'silo' working.

The Extended Schools Manager talked about the difficulties of working with and across agencies. Her skilful approach helped to pull these community-based services together to achieve what was emerging from the Extended Schools Board in terms of new local targets. These included numbers of families attending community events and, for families with higher needs, the number of families being supported by the CAF process. School leaders were gaining confidence in their new role as leaders of Extended Schools, as the promise of the twenty-first-century school emerged in 2008/9, meaning the potential to position schools as central to community services. They began to openly make judgements about Eastfield's LA and PCT/NHS centralized services. This fuelled a new tension between school leaders and Eastfield's strategic leaders. Perhaps the Extended Schools Manager's reference to developing this new approach as 'a ten year programme' was linked to managing and guiding partners on one hand to 'a common sense approach' but on the other hand to a radical local change programme.

Developing a new professionalism beyond partial understandings

Perhaps what seemed to be inherent tensions were a reflection of partial views and understandings of Orpintown's children and families. Each sector, whether primary or secondary schooling or voluntary or statutory agencies, had seemingly developed such partial perspectives of their service users based upon professionally and organizationally prescribed priorities. This was also reflected in the growing local agenda versus the traditional centralized Eastfield LA and PCT tension discussed in the previous section. After many years of these schools and community-based services working in that way, within their own practice, agency boundaries and measures of success, Extended Schools forced interests to be fundamentally challenged to construct new, shared ways of working with considerations of mutuality as central. The local Youth Work team was required to better understand the high school's perspective on the same young people with whom they both worked. Similarly schools started to understand that siblings may be in other schools and primary schools began to engage with practitioners in Early Years settings. These historically partial understandings of children and the new constructs of the same children that followed the revelations that these children were in close contact with other services and lived in families, served to challenge leaders and professionals alike. A new professionalism was being built that played out as these services came together, with learning from each other particularly evident in meetings. New holistic understandings of children resulted from the bringing together of a range of local, partial, views based historically on professional and organizational interest.

The Coalition and academization: No change on the front line
New understandings and working arrangements were being created as the partnership strengthened despite the Coalition signalling to schools that they should refocus their efforts on the classroom through a return to 'traditional educational values'. In 2011/12 another change of national policy impacted upon Orpintown. 'Successful schools' were being asked to convert to academies and free themselves from supposed local bureaucracies, severe reductions in public spending were being implemented and the key policies of Every Child Matters and Extended Schools, which were the mainstay of this partnership, were now being disregarded by the Coalition government. Orpintown had successfully created multi-professional working, which began to be recognized by the LA and was viewed as a potential model of good practice when the high school moved out of its longstanding relationship with the LA and became an academy.

The Academy hosted and led the partnership, so this move, seemingly towards an independent school being responsible directly to the DfE, raised concerns amongst primary schools and partner organizations. The newly appointed Extended Schools Manager followed the example of the previous post holder and worked extensively with partners to keep them engaged. The reality is that this fundamental change of the lead school's governance structure did not influence Orpintown's partnership. The Academy had learnt that it needed to maintain its work with primary schools and other partners to continue to improve standards and provide its pupils with the support they required and expected. Working mutually benefited children, their families and the community.

Conclusion
In 2007 Orpintown was known as a successful and confident community with high-performing schools and a strong market-town identity. The development of Extended Schools proved to be difficult despite these local strengths. The research revealed schools were largely working in isolation from each other, linked to the performativity agenda and there was also

a deep primary/secondary divide. Community-based organizations were similarly working to their own agendas. Each had to learn about each other's practice despite often working with the same children and families. Schools and these services worked with partial understandings of children and families. A highly skilled leadership figure was required to bring together this diversity of organizations.

It took several years for a new mutual understanding of children and families to develop, as there were many difficulties to be overcome at front-line and strategic levels. The high school assumed control of the agenda and based initial developments upon a deficit model of children, focused upon 'those children who were not educationally succeeding'. Against the odds the partnership began to thrive and construct new ways of working based upon more holistic understandings of children and families. This was a long journey that took many years. In 2011/12 the impact of the Coalition government's policies momentarily halted the partnership's development as New Labour policy of Extended Schools was disregarded and the high school converted to an academy. But those working in schools and community-based services had learnt these new partnership ways of working were things to be valued and retained.

Chapter 3
Gadley: Extended Schools building a new sense of community

Introduction
Gadley is the second Extended Schools partnership within Eastfield LA that contributed to this research. This chapter outlines the journey schools and community-based services adopted in Gadley to implement Extended Schools. Although similar guidance was provided by Eastfield LA to all its schools, Gadley's partnership developed in a different way to Orpintown. These different approaches demonstrate the flexibility of the Extended Schools policy framework and how it allowed localized responses to suit the needs of local communities.

Local developments were entwined with broader ambitions for schools than those contained in Extended Schools and Gadley's leaders went on to develop much more than a Core Offer. Residents of Gadley witnessed a new sense of community emerging as the partnership developed. Schools that took part in this research were collectively the largest employer locally and they became central to new service provision by coming together to forge new relationships with the community far beyond the constraints of parental choice and school performativity. Implementing Extended Schools brought about, for all concerned, a new understanding and consideration of children, their families and the community.

Gadley: the community and schools
Gadley is on the outskirts of Eastfield LA in a community that has long been associated with the coalmining industry. Gadley, although formally a village, by 2006 resembled a suburb of the city, with a high street and a range of services clustered around it. The high school is situated at the upper end of the high street, near a train station and with good transport links to Eastfield and the wider region. Both practitioners and local residents talked proudly of the heritage derived from the coalmining industry and the strong sense of local identity that linked villages together. Hence the

villages surrounding Gadley were frequently referred to as 'pit villages'. The last direct links with coalmining in the area ended over 20 years previously, with the closure of the pit, though some miners continued working in the industry, commuting to pits north of Gadley until these eventually closed.

A local resident, father and former pupil of the high school described his experience since the local schools had moved towards Extended Schools and provided hints as to how schools were revitalizing a local sense of community:

> There seems to be much less vandalism and kids hanging around since the schools opened up to do more things. My son comes here [the local school]. They do loads of things in holidays and he enjoys it. They are doing a club on a Friday night now. My son used to go off with his mates to god knows where. They come here; I know they are safe here. It also gives us a sense of identity. Since the pits around here shut, a lot of that has gone, but the schools are helping give us a local sense of community we used to have.

A brief outline of Gadley

A key feature of the area was the historical links with coalmining, leading to a large proportion of the population now being employed in family-based businesses that had developed as men lost their jobs in the mining industry. Residents discussed how these businesses were based upon skills developed both within the pits and the services that supported them such as electrical installation and general repair and servicing.

Statistics provided by the Eastfield LA indicated that Gadley is a relatively prosperous area with low unemployment. There is a mixture of owner-occupied housing and rented social housing. Although residents raised issues of small social housing estates where disadvantaged families lived, Eastfield LA's statistics suggested that, overall, there was little social deprivation. Residents reflected how Gadley had shifted from an independent community to become a commuter suburb of Eastfield and other cities in the region. Despite the growth in population attributed to commuting, the statistics showed a very low percentage of Black, Asian and Minority Ethnic families in the area. Similarly the 'new communities' emerging in many of Eastfield's schools, such as those from Eastern Europe or Africa, were not particularly evident. During the period of research a Children's Centre was built and opened in one of the villages where deprivation was higher. Overall unemployment remained marginal across the partnership's geographical area, although youth unemployment increased after 2010.

Respondents consistently referred to the sense of community but there was no secondary tier of local administration such as a town council to survive the reorganization of local government in 1974. The Miners' Welfare, which had developed to support miners and their families, was formally central to Gadley in terms of education, social, and financial support. It was the focus of the community providing activities for adults and children alike. Eastfield LA, as with Orpintown, provided all major local services to Gadley including Youth Services and Early Years. Health services were managed via the Eastfield PCT, which was changing to 'GP-led commissioning' towards the later stages of the research under the Coalition's reform of the NHS. Services such as police and fire were provided by the same regional bodies as delivered services to Orpintown.

The schools in Gadley and its surrounding villages

A high school and eight feeder primary schools came together to form Gadley's Extended Schools partnership. The governors of the high school talked of their pride in the performance of their school at Key Stage 4, with consistently good results. However they also described how these were not converted into comparably high results at A levels or access to higher education. School staff discussed the continued influence on the area of the coalmining industry and the comparatively low level of value attached to further education as a pathway through to universities and the professions. These staff went on to state that young people valued 'trades' and had ambitions to 'join the family business'. Despite this issue the high school's Ofsted reports by 2007 had progressed to the status of 'outstanding', which was maintained throughout the research. At Key Stage 4 this school was among the top-ranking schools in the country.

Predating Extended Schools, Eastfield Further Education College had successfully run an adult education programme in the schools. There was also a tradition of 'letting rooms' to community groups in all the schools and allowing the hiring out of the playing field to local sports clubs thus bringing the local community into schools on a regular basis. However, as we will see later, the leadership of Gadley schools thought such activities were merely 'tokenistic' and did not reflect their new ambitions, triggered by the Extended Schools policy, of 'true community schooling'. The high school's Parent Teacher Association (PTA) was described locally as 'having survived for many years' and was the historic link between the school and the community.

The primary schools enjoyed a similar high standard of performance; despite the odd exception in 2007, but most schools were judged to be good by Ofsted. In the main these were very popular schools, which had maintained strong links with their village communities. However the leadership of the high school was to heavily influence the primary sector in Gadley.

The services that contributed to local developments included the high school and its primary feeder schools, the Youth Service, the Early Years Service, Children's Social Care, the police, small local voluntary-sector organizations, and health services. The journey towards Extended Schools development in Gadley was a complex one. Gadley's school leaders had greater ambition for their schools than being merely successfully engaged in Extended Schools. They saw them as an integral part of the community offering much more than the Core Offer. The journey was one that intertwined this agenda with other national agendas that emerged as the research progressed.

Moving towards Extended Schools

When the research commenced in 2007 Gadley's schools were rapidly moving towards the formation of a comprehensive Extended Schools partnership linked to a shift of schools to Foundation School status. This status meant that the schools could take ownership of their lands and directly employ their staff. It represented a more independent form of governance than that of a traditional local authority school.

Schools forming a trust in parallel to Extended Schools developments

Gadley's schools were moving to Foundation Trust status in response to a further strand of New Labour's policy attempts to diversify the market in schooling. New Labour had introduced specialist school status for secondary schools and in their second term a new interim school structure of Foundation Trust. Gadley's primaries and the high school took this as an opportunity to shift away from their close relationship with the LA. They then formed their individual school trusts into a partnership trust. This partnership trust allowed them to share resources and act in close cooperation with each other. As the research progressed through 2008 Gadley's schools constituted a new overarching mutual structure named the 'Schools Trust'. But the research also indicated that its roots were directly related to new localized understandings generated initially through Extended Schools across the period 2006–7.

Table 3.1 Gadley Schools' Partnership Trust Board

Gadley Schools' Partnership Trust Board	
Key purpose of this structure	To bring schools together to work across Gadley with the aim to improve standards and engagement with the community as schools move to Foundation School status. This Board later moved to manage academies that joined Gadley's Academy Trust following the Coalition's promotion of academies.
Chair of the meeting	The Chief Executive of the Schools' Trust
Members included	School headteachers and governor representatives
	Partner Higher Education Institution
	The Learning and Skills Council
	Strategic Lead for Health
	Representatives of headteachers
	Police

Historic accounts from school and community-based staff revealed that the development of Gadley's Extended Schools partnership commenced in 2005 when the government first started to define its approach. The principal of Gadley's high school and governors debated the policy and its relevance to local schools and took the decision to 'grasp this agenda'. The school had described itself as a 'community school' but the deputy principal stated 'this is in name only', and the community use of facilities such as playing fields and classrooms and the PTA were repeatedly described as 'tokenistic'. The deputy principal of the high school admitted when the Extended Schools policy emerged that he 'really started working out there in the community and started to actively find out who was out there in the community and the kinds of roles and what they were'. But there was also a realization amongst school leaders that a new type of leader was needed to progress this new agenda.

Introducing new leadership skills to the school workforce

Gadley's schools had responded to the 'standards agenda' by developing a leadership based upon a largely inward looking school-based professionalism in response to schools working within a competitive market. This was apparent in both primary and secondary schools, though the primary sector seemed much more open to parents and the community when compared to secondary schooling. The high school took the lead on Extended Schools by seconding a highly experienced youth and community manager from the LA in 2005. The principal of the high school recognized the lack of community expertise in the staff team. This secondment was initially on a temporary basis. The Extended Schools Manager had a thorough knowledge of community education and community development and was able to help schools 'make sense of the community'. This manager commenced work on behalf of the schools in Gadley and supported the vice principal by firstly 'setting out to undertake a community audit'.

The Extended Schools Manager immediately hit problems with the schools' workforce on two fronts. Firstly: 'I think sometimes I can be seen as a threat' in terms of existing school philosophy and 'so to carry people [mainly teaching staff] and get them to understand we are not replacing academic excellence, we are adding to it and supporting it whilst making sure the community comes along with us. This is quite a challenge.' Second, in terms of the practicalities of residents using school resources 'sometimes teachers see pencils have moved on their desks ... at night a cooker had crumbs left on it ... teachers are very precious about their classrooms ... and the key is to talk it through because teachers feel threatened'.

The Extended School Manager, coming from 'a youth work culture', also noted how teaching staff worked and spoke about how she approached broadening their understanding: 'they have got trained to come to work with children in a certain way ... so we try to show them how we can complement the work they are already doing'. This new manager was starting to bridge Gadley's seemingly deep education and welfare divide.

Blurring education and welfare boundaries: Not a simple matter

Although primary schools were recognized locally to be orientated towards the community, the Extended Schools Manager spent many hours working with their leadership to engage them in a new approach to home–school relationships, broader than that previously understood by teaching professionals. The manager identified the need to engage all school leaders in this new agenda, which was much more community-orientated than Gadley's schools had been previously.

There were high school staff that could see the possibilities once the principal had 'grasped the opportunity' to engage in the new government's school agenda of Extended Schools. But a governor and parent from one of Gadley's primary schools, having observed the developing agenda locally, also became concerned about a potential tension between the Extended Schools agenda and the focus upon classroom and school standards: '[I was] seeing quite a divorce between the school and Extended Schools provision' and that while 'headteachers are "bought in" ... at individual governing bodies level you do not see anything of it'.

Whilst the Extended Schools Manager dealt with tensions of introducing a new perspective to schooling across Gadley, one of the teaching staff gave a strong warning about local school leaders approaches and their tendency to go headlong when introducing new ideas: 'it is a bit of a Gadley thing that we have strong leadership and once they have got the bit between the teeth, they are off!'

Engaging with the leadership and professionalism of schools was only one aspect the Extended Schools Manager had to tackle. Whilst the Extended Schools Manager came with 'a deep understanding of the community and its workings', being based in and working out of Gadley's schools meant she also had to engage with the professionals in the community in a new way. The deputy principal of Gadley high school set out an approach to 'blur boundaries between education and health and develop co-locate services', which proved in Gadley to be a radical agenda after a history of schools looking inward and being principally concerned with their standards agenda. Examples of this blurring of boundaries included joint working with the NHS and Youth Services and the partnership lead on developing Children's Centres in the area, combined with a team of Family Support workers based within schools.

Schools: Invisible within their community

Residents and managers of community-bases services said that schools had not been visible within the community for many years and as a result a consensus existed in the community's understanding of schools. Youth Service managers viewed schools as 'inwardly looking organizations and remote', linked to 'the school performativity agenda', and parents said they were 'self-interested organizations'. Local community-based professionals held concerns about the sudden surge of interest amongst school leaders in engaging with the community, but also about these same school leaders being placed, through the developing Extended Schools policy, as the leaders of these comprehensive partnership developments. Community-based services viewed the community as their territory.

But some community-based staff, such as the Children's Social Care Manager noted how, at a difficult time for her service, Extended Schools developments were assisting with safeguarding children:

> Our referral rates into Social Care leapt dramatically post the Baby P incident. Extended Schools gives us the opportunity to discuss some specific cases and some general principles and thresholds for referral into our service locally. I am particularly impressed by the stance they have taken with regard to children who attend the schools in the area who are known to social care.

Baby P was a 17-month-old boy who died from injuries in August 2007 following abuse from his mother and her partner. The national outcry with regard to protecting children from serious harm followed that relating to the case of Victoria Climbie.

But, conversely, the local youth worker saw a divide between the historical view of local schools and youth work interests regarding young people:

> Schools have their own values, opinions and attitudes. The young people actually self-exclude feeling they do not fit ... I am concerned if Extended Schools took over and there is no need for our programmes, which is one way it could pan out. Then I would be really concerned that the most disadvantaged and needy young people would miss out on an important service.

However, the youth worker noted: 'the partnership is school-led, but I do get a say in the Extended Schools meetings' and through negotiation with the Extended Schools Manager he realized a position through which

Extended Schools and the Youth Service could work side-by-side to benefit local young people:

> As a result of the Extended Schools partnership young people with issues like challenging behaviour or other needs have benefited … that gives us a balance between the universal services mainly provided by the school and targeted services provided by my service.

As schools had seemed 'invisible' in the community, some services, such as NHS staff, found it difficult to engage with schools. Others saw schools looking beyond their gates as something that provided a new challenge to them, but also might present an opportunity.

Inclusive governance arrangements to deliver new ways of working

The Extended Schools Manager commenced developing the governance framework in 2005, as illustrated in Table 3.2. Observation of meetings and discussions with the Extended Schools Manager and a diversity of agencies demonstrated that this approach to governance was based upon 'inclusive partnership principles', and updated constantly. Extended Schools group meetings took place 'as and when needed to aid the development of the [local] Extended Schools plan' alongside the construction of the 'local needs analysis' devised with the aid of partners.

A theme arose around a meeting culture and the contribution of potential partners to Extended Schools. The Extended Schools Manager noted that Gadley's partnership stood for action as opposed to the LA-led meetings, which she perceived to be characterized by inaction and consisted of: 'professional meeting attenders whose justification for existence appears to be they have to have another meeting … that arranging a further meeting was the only outcome'. She went on to explain: 'if you want to join the party [the partnership], services must tell us what they are going to contribute in the way of resources'. In forming the Extended Schools partnership and the later Schools' Trust, Gadley's schools did not wish to repeat what they judged to be Eastfield LA's wasteful approach to working. They wanted a partnership that represented players willing to develop and deliver successful actions, based upon community need.

Table 3.2 Gadley Extended Schools Board

Gadley Extended Schools Board	
Key aims of this structure	Overview of all developments of Extended Schools including localized working around families and the development of the Core Offer of services
Chair of the meeting	LA Senior Manager from Children's Social Care
Members included	Gadley's Extended Schools Manager
	LA Early Years Manager
	LA Youth Manager
	Primary schools staff and governors
	Parent representatives via schools
	NHS manager
	Police
	Mental health (children and young people's)
	LA Extended Schools Coordinator
	Voluntary service and charity representatives
There were no subgroups formed. To join, partners had to bring resources with them and sign up to a mutual method of working that empowered individual members to work within a broad framework.	

The highly skilled Extended Schools Manager, with a deep knowledge of communities and community-based services, sought also to build a structure that reflected a diversity of services. To this end she engaged with partners in meetings to ensure that the partnership fully reflected services that can respond to 'local need', and that no potential partners were left out. The inclusivity and valuing of partners was demonstrated by the nomination of an LA employee as chair and also by ensuring that 'all those who brought services to the table' were fully empowered with voting rights and considered equal to the school leaders that joined them in decision making. The Children's Social Care Manager who was also the Extended Schools

Gadley: Extended Schools building a new sense of community

Table 3.3 Gadley Extended Schools Board: a selection of services developed

> The services developed by Gadley Extended Schools Board included:
> - The facilitation of localized integrated multi-professional working around families – a radical shift in emphasis from crisis intervention associated with Children's Social Care to one of early intervention and prevention; including support for step down from Children's Social Care interventions into more universal services ensuring families. The latter ensuring a continuation of support for the family following Children's Social Care 'closing the case'
> - A coherent system of lettings for school premises and specialist areas such as sport fields and halls
> - International events for community and young people, including exchange visits of staff and pupils, to broaden understanding and share good practice
> - Community sports events to promote healthier lifestyles
> - Shaping and engaging organizations in the development of family support
> - Parenting courses to support the development of parental skills
> - Children and young people's involvement in the design and delivery of services
> - Closer working with the police to improve community safety
> - New services linked to counselling and young people's mental health
> - Developing community school shops staffed by pupils and open to the public
> - Local events and festivals including music and the arts
> - Before and after school facilities including breakfast and homework clubs
> - Supporting the development of local childcare – including a new Children's Centre
> - Work related to community and pupil health and well-being
> - Involving parents in their child's education
> - A range of universal youth work provision
> - Diversionary programmes aiming to reduce youth offending
> - Referral mechanisms with tracking system
> - Engaging with parents and the community in basic skills, FE, and HE activities

chair commented upon deep-seated self-interest of school leaders linked to school performance across the LA, and how Gadley differed:

> I got the feeling that other partnerships are swamped by headteachers and all in a bun fight there to make sure the needs and interests of their kids are being met ... I would say the partnership I chair is an exception. The chair is usually a headteacher, but ours is not ... therefore it is not a headteacher who is running it who has another hat on thinking of what is in the best interests of their school. And this is not in the best interests of kids in the locality.

Alongside developing these governance arrangements the Extended Schools Manager commenced developing a temporary multi-professional team based in the high school with 'the full support of the principal'. This expanded over the years 2005 to 2010 to become a permanent team that included the Extended Schools Manager (who was promoted to become a member of both the high school's leadership team and the Schools' Trust), a new youth and community worker and two family-support workers. The team, with the support of staff from other local community-based agencies, worked towards the delivery of the local Extended Schools plan and with the development of new local service provision, as outlined in Table 3.3. This new team based within the schools in the area added further knowledge and professional understanding to Gadley's schools' workforce. But despite this, the partnership faced many challenges whilst being developed.

Differing service priorities and changing professionalism
Aside from the continuing issue of gaining the trust of school-based staff, school managers were asked to shift from an inward-looking approach to one that could coordinate community-based services in a new way. A school governor voiced several times the issue of Extended Schools devising a parallel track to that of everyday school business. These comments implied that the emerging team and associated new activities were somehow not part of the schools' workforce but working separately to the schools. And perhaps that school governors remained more focused upon the governance and management of schools, rather than becoming involved in the changes taking place in the Gadley community triggered by the implementation locally of Extended Schools.

The issue of local emerging priorities that came through the strengthening partnership, such as the need for family support, were not always congruent with views held centrally by Eastfield LA and PCT. This caused conflict to develop with local staff responsible to city-wide organizations. A centralized LA Children's Plan with priorities different to Gadley's Extended Schools plan meant staff were being pulled in two directions. The youth worker met his Eastfield LA targets by working in partnership through schools running 'more universal youth-club type services' whilst he and his youth-work team focused upon more targeted work with young people who 'would not engage with provision such as that offered by the school'. Of this approach, which bridged local and LA demands, he said, 'I think young people get a lot more holistic services … that is from young people's feedback.'

While the youth worker was able to take advantage of the developing agenda, the School Nurse employed by Eastfield PCT worked with vulnerable children in the schools in Gadley. She noted how the PCT had changed her role from that of undertaking individual healthcare assessments, as these were now carried out by healthcare support workers, to one of working with children with higher identified needs. Of Extended Schools she said she became involved through a local event promoting this policy approach, however, other health professionals did not go 'so it is down to nurses who are interested'. For those who opted in: 'there is a fantastic relationship' but there were also contentious issues to overcome, an example being that 'we have a health bus, a mobile unit I work out of. We wanted the bus to go onto the high school car park … we park elsewhere because the school will not have it on their site.' The School Nurse attributed this to the links between sexual health and young people. This bus being sited on the school's car park could send out what she said was the wrong message to 'the community about pupils, from the school's perspective'.

The School Nurse and other local health professionals and their managers could see that eventually they may be managed by a school-based leadership and there were concerns about this. A health professional stated: 'if we were in school all the time we may get dumped with all the paracetamols and all that first aider type stuff … which might stop us doing the real health promotion stuff'. They also noted: 'many school nurses do not understand what is going on' and that there were limitations to how much senior managers from the PCT viewed Extended Schools as part of the community-based health professional's role. But in reality Extended Schools had provided Gadley a route through which 'relationships could be built. If you have not got that relationship with members of [school] staff, you really struggle to do your job.'

The ambition and drive of the schools to work together more mutually on a wider agenda than Extended Schools led to the aforementioned Schools'

Trust being established in 2008. This trust status allowed schools greater autonomy when compared to the typical LA school but it also allowed schools to join together and unify services, such as joint primary curriculum work and the development of community shops jointly owned by the Schools' Partnership. Gadley's schools opened and ran shops on the high street through which pupils could engage in work experience as well as broaden the profile of local schools within the community. Examples included school uniform and hairdressing shops. Extended Schools eventually came under this new structure with a further shared accountability consisting of LA, health services, police, HE strategic leaders sitting alongside school leaders to drive forward a much bigger agenda. The new ways of working across schools involved input from this broader range of leadership figures, who held offices on the trust. Perhaps this new, much broader approach to schooling was linked to school leaders' discovery of community-based services and the differing priorities they held and the wider understanding of childhood, set within the context of the family and community. Ambitions included restructuring all nine schools to become 'more effective units working truly collaboratively together'. To this end a new Director of Primary Education was established to 'support the primary schools with curriculum development and school improvement'. Further to this, functions such as administration were merged across both primary and secondary education.

Accounts from members of the community noted how the schools were shifting towards a collective approach whilst increasingly working with their new found partners in the community.

The Coalition and a new national policy emphasis

As Extended Schools continued to develop and thrive in Gadley the Coalition's emerging policy was to impact upon both the partnership and the schools themselves. Most of the schools that formed the Schools' Trust converted to academy status in 2011/12. The Schools' Trust changed into a body that could facilitate the newly emerging role of hosting groups of academy schools. As schools across the country converted to academy status they started to affiliate with this new organization, established by Gadley, which had the capacity to provide leadership and support. The chair of the Schools' Trust, now the Academy Trust, in 2013 described how it now had 'a huge sum of money to manage with school improvement at its centre' and to this end 'it outsources estate management, employs its own finance and Human Resource's people and moved its offices nearer to London. They are now at the cutting edge of reform under the Coalition government ... they are moving at a pace.'

Gadley: Extended Schools building a new sense of community

The process that started with the principal of the high school 'grasping the opportunity offered by Extended Schools' in Gadley in 2005 had led to a new organization forming, which served over 40 schools that had recently moved to academy status.

Tensions between the schools within the Extended Schools partnership arose due to this shift from a very local to a national agenda based upon academization. The Chair of the Academy Trust suggested in relation to emerging academy chains that 'the concept of the community school goes out of the window and that is regrettable'. This view appeared to reflect the fracturing of working relationships with local LAs as rapid academization took place up and down England, and as a result schools coming together to form national trusts where there was no apparent local focus. The formation of these national academy chains marked the loss of localized community relationships, schools seemingly becoming businesses resembling a chain of supermarkets with national interests, rather than local public services with a stake in the community. The trust's chair viewed this shift in relation to schools and their community as 'a disaster that has happened now and the direction that has been taken'. However he went onto explain the rationale behind this shift of Gadley's school leadership 'clinging to values and aspirations of the previous government will not take anybody anywhere'. The chair was referring to the localized dimensions of Extended Schools and the new partnership working that had emerged.

However, out of the bringing together of schools from around the country into the new trust, a new direction also emerged from Extended Schools. The Extended Schools Manager, who had become an assistant principal, reflecting the importance of this community agenda to Gadley's schools, gained further status. As the number of schools from across England joining the Academy Trust grew, Extended Schools started to play out within these newly converted academy schools. This resulted in the Extended Schools Manager becoming a National Specialist Leader in Education through being asked to advise academies about implementing an Extended Schools programme. Her skills in youth and community work and the learning from the development of Gadley's Extended Schools partnership were being shared with primary schools joining the Academy Trust. The Extended Schools Manager viewed 'the smart approach is to get the good practice of Extended Schools out there' but instead of using the original aim of developing a response to Every Child Matters at a local level, her approach changed to: 'helping as many as possible with the [Coalition] government's new focus on examinations'.

Her knowledge of services such as parental mental health and substance misuse and her associated understanding of children that went beyond 'purely school-based staff' was now being utilized across these academies to introduce a broader concept of childhood through which the aim was to further improve school standards. Hence the accent appeared to change from the broader perspective of New Labour's Every Child Matters agenda to that of the Coalition, with a refocus on exam results and league-table positions.

In 2013 dramatic changes in school governance, which occurred as a result of Coalition policy, meant Gadley's schools were now independent academies working with other academies up and down England. But nothing changed in Gadley as Extended Schools developments continued to thrive. The Extended Schools Manager discussed her role, which now included advising schools nationally:

> Brown [the former Prime Minister] talked of Every Child Matters and Extended Schools and everything that went with it. Now we have very little of that. I can't remember the last time I saw Every Child Matters on a piece of paper. So that has completely gone out of the window. There is much more focus now, certainly working in schools, purely around results. That is what results children get at Key Stages throughout their school career. I can imagine in some areas this has caused a huge problem for Extended Schools … now become deemed not so important but it has not affected us and we are being much more asked to support pupils to help them achieve their grades.

The Extended Schools Manager also discussed how multi-professional work was now everyday practice in Gadley. In 2014 she commented: 'we cannot see the days coming back again where everyone sits in their own little boxes [professional and organizational silos] and get on with their little thing … we will continue to develop new ways of working via Extended Schools'.

An analysis of the Gadley experience
Developing Extended Schools in Gadley proved to be a complex affair. This section will consider key themes that emerged from the research in Gadley.

Schools and their educators and a sense of community
Gadley was a community to whose identity coalmining had been central. Recent generations were losing this sense of heritage and community cohesion, as mines and associated heavy industries had closed. In reality

Gadley: Extended Schools building a new sense of community

Gadley had become a commuter community with many small family businesses. Schools emerged, through improved public investment in education, as the community's largest employer. A new sense of educator responsibility was emerging in the context of the community replacing the lost heritage of mining.

Gadley's deputy principal had considered 'tokenistic' calling his school a 'community school'. This tokenism apparently included the schools' workforce and its lack of community knowledge, despite the local heritage. This motivated the high school's principal and governing body to take the opportunity offered by the government's Extended Schools policy. A new leadership figure with knowledge of how communities work was needed in the form of a seconded youth and community manager, to help primary and secondary school leaders to engage with a community agenda. Government was constructing policies that gave school leaders permission to take responsibility for a much wider community agenda.

But, leadership training and guidance provided by bodies such as The National College of School Leadership, appeared to these school leaders as 'off the pace on the Extended Schools policy agenda'. The college was still training school leaders about issues internal to schools and focused upon managing 'technical processes' and of course optimizing standards. Interestingly, community residents understood this bigger agenda, one stating: 'If our community and our families are not functioning properly, then nothing else functions, including the local school'.

Widening the professionalism of the school workforce

Whilst school leaders welcomed further New Labour policy, such as 'the twenty-first-century school', which made school leaders responsible for developing multi-agency hubs in or around their schools, the deputy principal admitted to being on 'catch-up'. Local school leaders could see the potential of this new agenda in the context of Gadley but were ill-equipped to deal with it. The schools' workforce was also resistant to change as local schools were performing well and comfortably meeting Ofsted and league table requirements. The Extended Schools agenda was a new direction agreed by the principal and the governors of the high school and not set within the context of classroom practice, therefore seemingly irrelevant to the school workforce. It involved members of the community taking over classrooms and school equipment throughout the newly extended week and the challenge posed to the school workforce of engaging with new considerations of children and their lives outside the classroom. It also drew investment away from internal school resources and took staff out to work in the community. The Extended Services Manager successfully managed this conflict by working across the school and community divide. This included the primary schools that were also required to learn about children and families in a much broader sense.

The school and community divide revealed concerns, from school staff and governors, that a twin track or dual approach could develop, if within the classroom nothing changed while Extended Schools was being developed separate to everyday school activity. There was some evidence of this in the early days of constructing new provision. The Extended Schools team were working outside the context of Gadley's schools, as school leaders began to learn that to 'bring the welfare and education agendas together' involved much more than the co-location of services in or around schools. There was much learning to take place and new agendas to confront. The Extended Schools Manager made it clear: 'what we do not want in Extended Schools are trained teachers. We need to bring in people with new skills.' Perhaps having achieved 'outstanding status', school leaders may have thought that developing Extended Schools was a fairly simple task.

Schools' dedication to this agenda serves to dispel the notion that Extended Schools was a policy for so called 'failing schools' only and demonstrates that outstanding schools, such as those serving Gadley, also had more to learn about children. As school leaders started to get to grips with this new agenda a school teacher commented on the demise of the identity of the community and why Extended Schools were of such value to Gadley: 'Mrs Thatcher said there is no such thing as community [society] ... and had an emphasis on the individual. Maybe now what we are doing is a rebuilding of that [the community] through Extended Schools?'

This statement echoes that of Gadley's deputy principal who discovered through Extended Schools that 'we have a responsibility for the community and we do not take it lightly'. As the Extended Schools Manager commented in 2014, in terms of shifting school thinking over a nine year period:

> I hope that what started off as me nagging, screaming, yelling, cajoling, bribing and generally causing havoc around the place so that teachers would pay attention would now mean Extended Schools are everyday work. I am doing a session for all the schools' teachers which is like a sign off. That is what Extended Schools are. We are there now as opposed to when we started when school staff had no idea of what I was talking about.

An inclusive partnership valuing all

The skills of the Extended Schools Manager were ably demonstrated in devising a partnership that was inclusive and recognized potential partners as equals. The schools were clearly responsible for delivering new services, however governance and meeting arrangements were grown using a 'community development approach' that respected everyone's voice including parents, children, young people, and local residents.

There were two simple and openly expressed criteria to join the partnership: 'to bring resources, and not to engage in endless conversation in meetings'. The partnership was openly keen not to try to replicate a model they considered characterized that of the LAs. The partnership was centred around actions based upon local need. Some partners were able to contribute fully to this agenda; whilst others were held back by their senior management who considered Extended Schools irrelevant to their service, such as sections of the PCT and NHS who were not fully on-board with this local agenda. And some were concerned about an eventual longer-term takeover of their roles by schools.

Gadley's leadership rapidly moved to merge schools who had adopted a much broader agenda than that presented by Extended Schools. Schools' functions were integrated within the Schools' Trust and provided an umbrella organization consisting of leaders of not just schools but other services, under which Extended Schools could also be governed. But this in turn spawned an even larger agenda to develop through the Coalition's academization programme. Some 40 schools joined a new Academy Trust from across England, which was considered by some as a threat to the localized agenda, but also proved to be an opportunity for the Extended Schools Manager to work across the country developing partnerships between schools and communities.

The Coalition: Little influence on the approach to Extended Schools

Despite the schools in Gadley shifting in 2011 towards the Coalition's agenda of academization of schools and the enthusiasm of Gadley's high school leaders to develop a national academy chain, Extended Schools had become increasingly embedded in Gadley and tensions between schools and broader services lessened. Partners valued the approach, which included a pathway to further improve school standards. The Coalition's disregard for Extended Schools and the associated Every Child Matters agenda, and its emphasis on a return to 'traditional educational values' delivered through the technical processes of classroom practice, had little if any influence upon a thriving local partnership. The Extended Schools Manager crucially shifted her language from that of New Labour and their policy scripts, such as Every Child Matters, to one of Extended Schools contributing to improving standards. Extended Schools was now part of everyday work. Residents supported this stance commenting: 'The [primary] school has become an integral part of the community it serves. It is much more than a school to us now' and '[the high] school is the hub of the community and I am sure most people agree it is the biggest thing we have'. It appears that Gadley's leaders chose eagerly to move on the Coalition's academization programme, yet they had learnt the value of New Labour's Extended Schools approach.

Perhaps this long journey was one that also concerned replacing the miner and the pit with the educator and schools, to provide future opportunities for residents and upon which to realize a new shared identity for Gadley.

Conclusion

Gadley's school leaders saw the Extended Schools policy as an opportunity through which they could fulfil a commitment to the community. The schools' workforce had focused upon internalized processes that delivered outstanding schools, but it was ill-equipped to deliver this new agenda. Delivering Extended Schools was to be a long-term project led by the creation of a new role which required a manager with high skills levels and in-depth understanding of the community and the organizations that work in it. This appointment carried full support of all Gadley's school leaders.

But there were conflicts that emerged that reflected differing professional and leadership perspectives. In particular the schools' workforce could not see the relevance of this new direction, causing some dissention to emerge, as Extended Schools developed in parallel until teachers' views were changed. The diminishing sense of the 'mining community' appeared to be linked with the development of Extended Schools as schools moved to become the hubs of the community with ever more ambitious plans to merge with each other. In some ways this ambition and its nine years of development was challenged by the Coalition but through the Academy Trust new opportunities were opened-up for more schools, who sought to engage with Extended Schools as a route through which to improve standards.

Chapter 4
Hayfield: Extended Schools legitimizing schools' approach

Introduction
Chapters 5 and 6 will be concerned with two further Extended Schools partnerships, which were within Farrington Local Authority. This chapter will focus on a partnership of schools located in a rural community which was described by all concerned as enjoying a good lifestyle with a few pockets of rural poverty. The partnership started to work towards a broader agenda akin to the Every Child Matters policy, prior to this central government initiative. A much broader agenda than that associated with school standards and league-table positions seemingly was everyday work in Hayfield. New Labour policy such as Every Child Matters and Extended Schools served to verify these schools' direction of travel, as opposed to driving it.

Two key themes will emerge that motivated Hayfield's approach to children, young people and families. Firstly there was a key leadership figure, the high school's principal, who believed that schooling involved a more holistic philosophy than that of school performativity. And secondly, as the schools in Hayfield engaged in early intervention and prevention strategies, they were able to identify pupil and family need, or as they referred to them, 'barriers to children's learning'. But in this rural setting, services to meet these needs were in short supply, causing the schools to create their own multi-professional team. This model of Extended Schools was recognized by all concerned as being successful in a fairly wealthy collection of rural villages. As we will see, the model was transposed and also improved standards within an inner-city community.

Hayfield: the community and schools
Hayfield is a relatively large village with smaller villages clustered around it on the fringes of Farrington LA. The village is one hour on public transport from Farrington town, which is the administrative centre for the LA. The town hosts a range of services for families, which local residents

and school staff said were not available in Hayfield and its surrounding villages. The high school and on-site public sports facilities represented the largest single community focus outside of the collection of small public buildings such as the council offices along Hayfield High Street. A parent at a meeting appeared to grasp the issue that Hayfield's schools had been reflecting upon: 'I think though it needs to be clear what our schools are for in the long run. Are they about academic subjects or are they about broader things?'

A brief outline of Hayfield

Hayfield shared the same local authority as Newtown Federation, the fourth case-study, to be introduced in the next chapter. The area enjoyed high levels of affluence, however, statistical data provided by Farrington LA also identified small pockets of multiple deprivation. Of the nine primary schools in the villages around Hayfield, featured in this research, one served a small community dominated by social housing and accompanied by high levels of deprivation. This community campaigned to build a new Children's Centre, which opened whilst the field research was taking place.

The high school's catchment covered a very wide geographic area, as there was little in the way of high concentrations of housing, compared with neighbouring cities where schools of a similar size could serve one or two local neighbourhoods. Other than the newly commissioned Children's Centre, respondents said the schools in the area were unable to access additional funding as the overall indicators of social deprivation were low when compared to other schools in the same local authority. As a result the development of Extended Schools in this area relied upon a small and temporary grant via the LA to support the development of services to fulfil the Extended Schools 'Core Offer'.

Residents from these villages discussed how almost everyone of working age commuted to employment in the local towns and cities in the region. Farrington LA's statistics illustrated unemployment and poverty were on the whole of little significance and suggested low levels of Black, Asian and Minority Ethnic residents and little in the way of 'new communities' in the area, as found in other parts of Farrington LA. These statistics reflected local residents' comments, that it was an area consisting of villages of 'white middle-class communities'. But school staff also commented on the small minority who were viewed as 'poor', seemingly being at a bigger disadvantage when compared to disadvantaged families living in inner city communities. Their view, summed up by a teacher, was linked to the issue of there 'being very few additional support services available in the area, other than through local schools, and the stigma attached to poverty in a wealthy community'.

Other infrastructure issues affected residents and particularly children and young people, and many comments were passed about 'things normally taken for granted', such as regular public bus services. The bus to the villages from the high school ran 'twice per day' and this around conventional school times of 8.30 a.m. and 3.30 p.m., and in some of the villages where primary schools were sited there was no bus service at all. Research participants considered this to influence parental choice for children to partake in activities such as before- or after-school clubs, unless other transport provision was put in place, either by the schools or parents, allowing children to access this part of the Extended Schools 'Core Offer'.

Hayfield's schools

The Hayfield Extended Schools partnership consisted of a high school with nine infant and junior schools spread across a large rural area. The schools in the Hayfield area were oversubscribed due to high demand and all were considered by local residents as 'very good schools'. All the schools visited had an air of 'openness', one example being how pupils walked freely between facilities in the high school without being escorted or challenged by staff. In other high schools that participated in this research, high levels of security were commonplace with electronic control mechanisms installed around the schools, controlling entry and exit points. The high school, despite having over 1,200 young people on roll, appeared very calm and quiet on each visit as did all the other schools in Hayfield.

Primary schools in the partnership retained the LA's preferred approach of separate infant and junior schools so these mainly 'one form entry' organizations were relatively small compared to other primary schools which took part in the study. The junior schools acted as 'natural feeders' for the high school. The infant and junior schools were established to serve both Hayfield and its surrounding villages. The schools were consistently judged by Ofsted as being 'good to outstanding', between 2003 and 2014. The principal of the high school, who led the Extended Schools partnership, reflected upon the ability to examine new ways of working as there was not the pressure upon performance many other schools experienced in 'constantly chasing improvement' in the context of 'Ofsted judgments and school league-table positions'.

Staff openly discussed the potential for schools in the area to move from their traditional relationship with their LA to one of Foundation Trust School and, when the Coalition came to power, to convert into academies. However, they resisted change and remained LA schools throughout the period of the research. A privately-run nursery on the high school site supported both the school staff and residents in the village with childcare. Similar arrangements were made within the villages where primary schools were located. These private providers represented the bulk of non-school services available to families in Hayfield, as there was little in the way of LA or NHS resources for children or families other than the statutory services of schooling and local medical centres that mainly consisted of GP practices.

As a result, unlike other Extended School partnerships that took part in this research, there were fewer, less diverse research participants with whom to engage. The participants that contributed to data collection included staff from the schools, encompassing the various dimensions of the multi-professional team, LA staff such as those from the Youth Service and a manager of a private nursery. Despite attempts to locate voluntary sector organizations none were found in the Hayfield area to support families. However, as will be seen, the Extended Schools partnership actively led localized working with other community-based voluntary services.

Moving towards Extended Schools

Prior to the research commencing in 2007, Hayfield's schools were committed to a very broad engagement with children, families, and the community. This was not the result of a response to national or local government pressure, nor a pressure to improve the schools' performance.

School leaders with wider community-centred ambitions

Interviews with a range of primary and secondary school staff revealed that the principal of Hayfield High had been for some time the driving force for schools to engage with the notion of developing broader services. This leadership figure viewed schools in the context of a much wider agenda than that defined through the Education Reform Act 1988 and the associated approach of school performance. Whilst DfES was starting to consider schools to potentially have a broader local role, such as the Full Service School pilots (DfES 2002), some five years before this research commenced

Hayfield: Extended Schools legitimizing schools' approach

Hayfield's schools were well along a pathway including the construction of on-site multi-professional teams. The principal referred to central government policy:

> It was the Every Child Matters agenda that really catalysed us, although we were working on the agenda before that. It was not totally new. When it came in, in 2003, I warmly welcomed that agenda because we had previously been charged with just the education agenda [as headteachers]. We know many children won't work at their best until a lot of wider issues are addressed. Until that child is comfortable about themselves they will not progress educationally.

Farrington LA recognized Hayfield schools as Extended Schools in their first round of awards in 2005. Despite the schools being described by LA managers as 'fairly leafy lane', these same managers considered these schools were 'well ahead of the game'. A school teacher commented of Hayfield's approach that: 'Every Child Matters is for every child and that is our foundation'. The philosophy that lay behind this adoption of broader working with children was explained by a number of school teachers as taking an 'early intervention and prevention approach' as opposed to 'looking at the end problems'. To support this statement a teacher cited young people leaving school with no employment, further education or training, or 'NEET' as they referred to it, and how they aimed to prevent this situation rather than simply working with them when they had become 'NEET'.

Accounts from a range of school-based staff and a LA-employed youth worker confirmed the adoption of this early interventionist approach within the local schools, and particularly in relation to the high school. In later chapters the differing cultures of primary and secondary schooling in relationship to the community will be discussed. Overall this research suggested that secondary schools have a tendency to look within themselves as organizations, as opposed to considering themselves part of a wider community, and those working in the primary sector were more likely to be community orientated. But in Hayfield it was clear that the high school was the local leader in community-orientated work. An Associate Headteacher from the high school further outlined the partnership's approach: 'Every child has always mattered. Children have never just brought their brains to school. They bring all sorts of issues to schools and we [school staff] have to make sure that we meet their needs.'

This Assistant Headteacher regarded all schools in the area as having the fundamental history and principles of 'working with other agencies and the community' and the introduction of the concept of Extended Schools by the LA as something 'we have always done a lot of as pupils are not islands; they live with parents and in the community'.

By 2008 the principal and leader of the Extended School partnership was described by a deputy headteacher as:

> ... heavily involved in activities within the community. He attends community meetings, runs breakfast and lunchtime working meetings with employers, churches, community leaders and has a good understanding of the community and its needs in the broadest sense.

This commitment of school leaders towards the community continued to expand until the conclusion of the research.

Schools leading multi-professional working

A multi-professional team funded by the partnership of schools had grown from initially employing one part-time counsellor/support professional in 2002 to include by 2006 a team of five staff who were able to respond to pupils' health issues including mental health, personal counselling, careers, employment, parental support, and teenage pregnancy. The team evolved in response to the identified needs of children and families, as 'we say every child matters, and we strive for the best for every child'. This broadening of services included 'before and after school clubs' and understanding community need 'through getting to know our families'. Table 4.1 summarizes the key activities of the team. An example of this breadth of engagement, cited by a junior school headteacher, involved:

> ... being approached by a mother who was in debt. She did not know what to do. I did not know where to start but I helped her work it out. I find personally we now cover much wider areas, lots of different ones as Extended Schools has progressed. It is in this way that schools are taking a greater role in the community and becoming the centre of communities.

When the field research commenced in 2007 the Extended Schools partnership had already added to the multi-professional team by employing 'a child and family specialist nurse' who talked of supporting families in whatever way they needed. The nurse worked with families in the community and invited them also into the school. Her role included a broader family approach than that of traditional 'school nursing', including sexual health advice, friendship advice, parenting support, and linking with local GPs and NHS services, Children's Social Care and a range of paediatrics services. Referring to the Every Child Matters and Extended Schools agendas in the context of LA and NHS service responses, she discussed how 'nothing has changed on the ground [referring to services external to the schools] but locally it has become the schools that have put things in place to continue to meet these agendas'; and 'we work well together' as schools in the area contributing to these services.

The careers and employment co-ordinator from the schools' multi-professional team discussed how communication had improved with parents over recent years. Some of the schools' processes were becoming better understood by parents and in particular school staff explaining issues like 'school reports to improve parental understanding of their child's progress ... that is something we are getting better at, contact with parents'. As a result home–school relationships had improved markedly. Another example she highlighted was the issue of praise. Some children had little value of their achievements and so she supported some parents with this important approach where 'kids are not used to parental praise'.

Table 4.1 Hayfield Schools, multi-professional team

A localized multi-professional team was established by schools, which consisted of a broad range of functions to meet local needs:
• Personal pupil counselling
• Health work in its broadest sense
• Employment and skills
• Family support

A consensus emerged from interviews with teaching staff and these professionals newly introduced to the workforce, that 'barriers to learning' were being overcome in a variety of ways to improve pupil outcomes. These included traditional school measures and the broader well-being of families, in areas from teenage pregnancy through to family break-up. A selection of new services introduced by the Extended Schools partnership can be found in Table 4.2.

Table 4.2 Hayfield Extended Schools: a selection of services developed

The services developed by Hayfield Extended Schools included:
- The facilitation of localized integrated multi-professional working around families – a radical shift in emphasis from crisis intervention associated with Children's Social Care to one of the early intervention and prevention; including support for 'step down' from Children's Social Care interventions into more universal services
- Before- and after-school activities including breakfast and homework clubs
- The community farm – employment and training opportunities for young people
- The community farm – volunteering opportunities for members of the community
- Employment and training events for young people
- The development of the local sports facility into a community enterprise – community ownership and management of the service
- Family support
- Parenting courses
- Parents understanding and participating in their children's education
- Confidential counselling for children and young people
- Volunteering schemes for young people
- Volunteering programmes for adults
- Community health events
- Expanded adult education programme
- Further use of schools by the community, e.g. community group meetings and self-help groups
- Supporting the development of a new Children's Centre
- A community skills bank – supporting the exchange of skills without money payments
- Community arts, music, and sports festivals
- Financial advice for parents
- Money matters for pupils
- Young people's leadership development
- Bringing together agencies to support families in need
- The development of a Hayfield Community Forum – to coordinate community developments – far wider than the Extended Schools Core Offer

Hayfield: Extended Schools legitimizing schools' approach

Central government policy legitimizes schools' approaches

As the research progressed, a growing confidence was exhibited by Hayfield's schools in their community-based approach. This direction was also becoming increasingly legitimized by central government policies. Leadership figures recognized the government's increasing emphasis on the intention to make schools the central focus of their community and its services, as outlined in the Children's Plan (DCSF, 2007a). An infant school headteacher noted that Farrington LA felt it no longer needed to defend locally the shift from narrow aspects of school leadership to those concerning community-based partnerships, as it had become evident that the Hayfield's schools were leaders in the region. The principal of the high school agreed with his primary colleague and talked of the barriers to further development of Extended Schools and the associated theme of multi-professional working. Hayfield's school leaders discussed the concept of the twenty-first-century school representing governmental approval of their work and providing national permission to drive their work further forward. The Hayfield partnership was setting the pace and school staff confidently stated that the LA and PCT were lagging in their response to this new local development of the Every Child Matters agenda. A school leader commented upon seemingly being held back:

> No matter how innovative the particular headteacher may be, if other services around them are not minded or not feeling the same way on joined-up work, then I think it is difficult for one manager in that locality to move it forward.

Schools embracing a community development role

A key motivation for schools in Hayfield to join together prior to the emergence of Every Child Matters and Extended Schools policies was closely linked to their geographical location. Children and family needs were being assessed by the schools, who found there was a lack of services in the immediate area to respond and that this in turn was 'acting as barriers to children's learning'. A high school teacher discussed how the few services available meant 'meaningful improvements for families were not easy to achieve'.

These factors, alongside the principal's drive to put schools at the centre of the community, brought about higher levels of engagement in Extended Schools than that of the Core Offer. Hayfield schools took ownership of a local smallholding and established a parent-led support group to maintain the facility which opened up new opportunities for local children to learn and gain new experiences. In 2009 the Extended Schools partnership took over the running of the local sports centre. The LA had planned to close the facility as reductions in public funding started to bite. In response, this failing sports centre was turned into a successful community enterprise in the later part of the research. The services provided by the Extended Schools Partnership by 2013 had developed to the extent that their Sports Partnership now covered the entire Farrington LA area. This was followed by the construction of a new young people's volunteering agency, which gained recognition and funding and has become a national centre for developing young people's leadership.

Perhaps the key strategic development for the Hayfield community was the conversion of the Extended Schools Breakfast and Lunch Business Meeting, outlined in Table 4.3, to become 'the Hayfield Community Forum'. This forum brought together the village communities and established a strong local voice for the area as well as being a mechanism through which further ambitious projects started to be constructed. Examples include an international sports event that was supported on its journey through Hayfield and more significantly for local families a 'food bank' and volunteering scheme framed around the concept of 'time bank'. The latter involved secondary school pupils and local residents volunteering to carry out tasks for other residents in exchange for time credits, through which these volunteers could ask for services in return. Despite the national agenda changing with the loss of Every Child Matters from the Ofsted framework and the Coalition's stance of ignoring the Extended School policy developments, the principal of the high school noted:

> We have continued to deliver the Extended Schools agenda. The LA seems very supportive of what we are trying to do. Because of the difficult period the LA has gone through financial issues and so on [2010–2014] they have pretty much left us to get on with it.

At the completion of the research in 2014 schools had moved far beyond the Extended Schools Core Offer to become crucial players in the community of Hayfield and the villages that surround it.

Table 4.3 Hayfield Extended Schools Breakfast Business meeting

Hayfield Extended Schools Breakfast Business meeting	There were no formalized governance arrangements in place to develop Extended Schools other than this meeting
Chair of the meeting:	High School principal
Members of the meeting included:	Headteachers from five infant schools
	Headteachers from four junior schools
	Faith organizations
	Community leaders
	Community and voluntary sector groups
	Local business leaders
	LA representatives
	Childcare providers

An analysis of the Hayfield experience

A number of key themes emerged through this longitudinal research as Hayfield schools pressed forward with their mission to develop a key position within their community.

Inspired leadership not governmental policy pressure

Hayfield schools had moved from the narrow internalized practice often associated with the standards and school improvement agenda to embrace a much wider approach to children. This had occurred prior to the commencement of the research in 2007. Historical accounts from school staff dating back to 2002 described how schools in the area were working in partnership and establishing a broad approach to education, predating government policy and guidance that emerged later in that decade. The schools' family nurse said: 'I don't think Extended Schools has changed my role at all', whilst a teacher referring to the same issue stated: 'what we have got set up is brilliant', and a pupil support services coordinator said: 'I think we were ahead of the game', referring to the Every Child Matters agenda. A shared view emerged from the schools, and was confirmed by LA staff, that Hayfield's partnership was having their approach to children and families affirmed by government policy as opposed to being led by it.

Analysis of the data strongly suggested that the principal was the key leadership figure who drove forward this shift in thinking across the high school, the primary schools and the community. Community figures talked of the principal's excellent understanding of the community, the issues families face and towards the end of the research he had become known as one of the community's key leadership figures. Farrington LA's management considered the principal in the same way and had great respect for the approach developed in Hayfield. At a time when schools were in competition with each other in the market for pupils and for league-table positions, there was a clear understanding that 'every child and every family mattered'. When parents were asked to compare their experiences of local schooling with those of their children they revealed:

> 'The schools have a much broader role now than in the past. They are concerned with broader things such as health issues.'

> 'I don't think schools are like they used to be, that is about academic work. They are involved in much more.'

> 'I think they look at parents a lot more than they used to do and I appreciate that. They are more open, you can come and talk to them.'

Schools much more valued locally than merely for league-table positions

Parents felt they were very fortunate to access these schools, not merely because of the high status of schools in terms of performance, but also because of their approach to family and community issues. 'As a parent if you have a problem you can come into school' said one local parent and further commented 'I think they get the whole picture and not just about a child knowing how to read and write'. These parental accounts confirmed the historic descriptions provided by school staff of an early shift towards very broad and inclusive perspectives on the child, family and local community, namely the adoption of an early intervention and prevention approach. Observations of morning staff meetings that took place in the schools emphasized this stance with an example being teachers, learning mentors, classroom assistants, and school leadership engaging in intensive dialogues about individual pupils and 'the issues they may face that day' as opposed 'to waiting for problems to arise'.

So why were these 'leafy lane schools', as one member of staff described them, which faced relatively minimal social issues when compared to some inner city schools, adopting an approach that reflected one laid out in emerging New Labour policy such as the Full Service School? The principal, the key driver in moving towards schools working more broadly, disclosed that early career experiences as a newly qualified teacher had 'broadened my outlook in terms of the issues families face, when compared to my formal teacher training'. He considered policy and practice guidance associated with schooling was often placed in separate boxes but that 'Extended Schools fitted well with my philosophy … these are not separate initiatives, but all one that can be grown, cared for, nurtured and that is what we are about' and 'that is the children's services offer which is centred around school sites through schools working together in groups or federations'.

And of his holistic approach he said:

> Needy and vulnerable children who are a small minority in this school are in a way more disadvantaged than say their peers who may be very upwardly mobile and more emotionally mature young people. So by that comparison life can be quite difficult and in some ways their needs are more pronounced.

Seemingly this approach was neither motivated by policy or training or requirements placed upon the schools but was the expression and development of a personal leadership philosophy concerning what education is and what the role of schools should be. Hayfield's community valued this approach.

Scarcity of community-based services to support local need

Alongside leadership principles, the issue of the rural location of the schools emerged as a second key theme that seemed to motivate the development of schools being open to a wide engagement with the community. Staff both from schools and the few services that were delivered in the community talked of children's needs being identified but a lack of capability to respond locally. This was attributed to the schools' location away from Farrington town where most services were sited and the affluence of the community, which meant that it drew down few if any additional services or funding other than the universal offer of schools and GP surgeries. Children who were at risk of harm were referred to Children's Social Care; however staff discussed how remote this service was and that despite rigorous assessment 'schools were usually left with the issue'. Staff from both the primary and secondary sectors were frustrated by the lack of response from the LA and health services to meet identified need. Further to this issue was a universal frustration with broader services that 'ring you up and want to know everything and do not always come back to you' leaving schools 'still dealing with the child and the issues'.

Headteachers were constantly making decisions in relation to school budgets to support children in this broader context. The high school's principal wrestled with the question of 'the narrower school standards agenda' compared to 'the broader identified needs of Hayfield's children' arguing:

> Do you go for hard targets you have been set to achieve? If you are single minded about it that is an agenda that could be followed in a school like this and leave a few 'dead bodies' along the way. The big issue is the emotional support etc ... but because you prioritize your drive for the academic achievement agenda those children could not access the support they needed. It is a hard one to manage in a school like this. Some [inner] schools have specific funding streams that are targeted towards this sort of agenda; this school does not have any of these. It is a harsh reality as Every Child Matters has come to be part of Ofsted [in 2007]. In terms of whether your school is outstanding, good or satisfactory it will come back to examination results and not this wider agenda.

The Coalition: 'traditional schooling' or continue with 'broader approaches'

Hayfield schools continued with their broader agenda despite the Coalition's education policy focusing upon 'traditional educational values' and dismissing the broader children's agenda as part of schools' concerns. Hayfield's school budgets remained central to supporting localized multi-professional teams. The principal in 2013 discussed the pressure on schools to respond to the Coalition's agenda, commenting that 'Every Child Matters as an initiative and a philosophy is very, very important because we should not be making all our decisions for children around academically based criteria reflecting our league-table concerns'.

The Extended Schools developments also spawned the broadening of the curriculum content of Hayfield's schools. Towards the conclusion of the research it emerged that much broader experiences continued to be offered to all pupils in the form of local provision outside the school gates, such as the community farm and sports centre, which also positioned schools strongly in the community. These schools were the largest pieces of public infrastructure in Hayfield and other villages. The community used these facilities to the extent where what started as an Extended School breakfast business meeting to aid development issues locally became the Community Forum encompassing multiple dimensions of the community, far beyond the children's agenda. A school leader summed up the position: 'we love to see our schools used during the day, evenings and at weekends by the community'. Schooling in Hayfield 'is not about children only, it is about their family and our community'.

Extended Schools: transferable leadership approaches

One may consider that in communities like Hayfield where poverty remained at low levels despite the economic recession and where school performance was high, moving forward successfully with Extended Schools may not have been that challenging. The principal noted in 2009 that as high-performing schools the pressure of league tables was not his sole preoccupation, so perhaps one could argue that Hayfield schools had the luxury of space to successfully develop Extended Schools. In 2011 Farrington LA awarded Hayfield's leadership with control of a challenging inner city 'failing school'. Hayfield's principal discussed the progress of this school over the years 2011–14: 'at Kent Trust School we have taken Hayfield's values and approaches and we have transposed them into a very different kind of school. But we have seen very rapid improvement within this school in all aspects.'

This holistic community-based approach was improving standards rapidly in an inner city 'failing school' and as the research closed Ofsted cited the principal and the new leadership team as 'creating a school where students feel valued and believe they can succeed'. Two key themes were deployed to achieve this improvement. Firstly the adoption of school improvement processes linked to classroom practices that were everyday business in Hayfield High. Secondly a comprehensive engagement with pupil's families and the local community so that the school's workforce could start to understand broader conceptualizations of their pupils. The principal considered, as with Hayfield, that both aspects were of equal importance. This demonstrated that the principles adopted in Hayfield towards Extended Schools, a fairly wealthy rural area, were also of value within challenging inner-city schools.

Conclusion

The Hayfield partnership of schools had adopted broader and more holistic approaches to their pupils and families prior to central government's development of Every Child Matters and Extended Schools policies. During the period 2003 to 2010 New Labour progressively attempted to engage schools with a new leadership role that considered children in the context of the family and community. This move merely affirmed the direction of travel already taken at Hayfield. The principal, while recognizing the importance of school performance, also viewed his role as much more than school standards and league-table positions. Over ten years he led the development of this partnership approach, which eventually converted the Extended Schools partnership into a much broader role as Hayfield Community Forum.

There was a perceived mismatch between the needs of children and families in this rural setting and the ability to successfully deliver appropriate support, based upon early intervention and prevention principles. Schools felt they had to create a multi-professional team to support families. As the largest pieces of infrastructure in the villages, schools became central to an agenda encompassing much more than the Core Offer required by New Labour's policy approach. The Coalition in 2010 effectively dropped the Every Child Matters and Extended Services policies but Hayfield's schools continued with this holistic, community-orientated agenda and further expanded it with the support of the community. Between 2011 and the conclusion of the research Hayfield's approach was successfully transposed by the same leadership to an inner city school facing severe challenges. It resulted in immediate improvements in pupil performance and well-being. This approach was not only for high-performing 'leafy lane' schools.

Chapter 5

Newtown: Extended Schools and a community rebuilding itself

Introduction

Newtown Extended Schools partnership is the second case-study within Farrington LA and the fourth and final case-study. This chapter will track backwards in time to 2002, when the three Newtown schools started the long process of coming together and looking beyond their school gates. As we will see, Newtown estate has experienced high levels of deprivation and at the millennium its schools were threatened with closure. 'Poor school league-table positions' accompanied by Ofsted inspections that concluded pupils were experiencing 'unsatisfactory educational opportunities' fed this view of both failing schools and a failing community.

This chapter engages in understanding how these three schools eventually merged to become a 'through school' covering ages 3 to 16 years and the long and arduous journey they undertook to develop a successful local multi-professional partnership, which became integral to new ways of working. It reveals how long-term vision and an approach that put families before organizational and professional interests contributed to schools becoming 'successful' in terms of measures of school performance, alongside a growing sense of the community's confidence in themselves and education. This transformation opened the potential for new opportunities for its residents.

Newtown: the community and schools

Newtown estate comprises a community of mixed social and private housing on the outskirts of a large town. Although the estate is attached to the suburbs of Farrington town, it was considered by research participants to be a community largely isolated from other neighbourhoods. Residents attributed this isolation to geographical and environmental factors and to an infant, junior and high school that solely serviced this community.

A brief outline of Newtown

Farrington LA had long held concerns about Newtown and its residents. It provided documents, at the commencement of the field research, that indicated low levels of community confidence coupled with multiple deprivation. Further documentary analysis enhanced this perception of an isolated community with a number of small community centres and shops. Despite a mixture of housing, most of the community consisted of social housing dating back to the 1940s.

The community of Newtown experienced rising levels of unemployment as traditional industries shrank in the 1970s and 1980s. Conversations with residents, supported by LA statistics, revealed this left the majority of families dependent upon state benefits. Statistics showed high levels of Black, Asian and Minority Ethnic families lived on the estate, compared with neighbouring estates. There was also an issue with transient residents who were said to 'come and go', alongside families who had lived in the community over many generations. A longstanding community worker, resident and former pupil of the local schools stated that this led to the prolonged presence of a local authority 'regeneration team, based in the local church to respond to local need'. She also commented on the local schools, in the context of a community that historically placed little value on schools and education, which was attributed to the culture of 'living on state benefits'. This community felt it had not shared in the growth in wealth of Farrington or the growth in new skills to match new types of local employment opportunities. Although of recent experiences linked to schooling, she added that:

> ... our work has been influenced by Extended Schools, definitely. The benefits of it are the work in the community. You know the kids' parents. The outcome is improvement in grades because of the work out of the school. Working not just in a school base, other places as well, all helps with the relationship with the schools. It has helped that relationship between the community and the schools.

Newtown's schools

Discussions with council managers illustrated that Farrington LA had a tradition of building a number of schools on single large plots of land in a way that allows each school to retain their individual identity. Different access routes into the infant, junior and high schools were constructed so that each was viewed as a separate organization. The schools in Newtown follow this pattern, with an adult education centre, an infant school, junior school and high school all built at various stages on a large shared site, fairly central to the community and surrounded by housing. Despite being on one large site, their positioning did not reflect the more recent trend of a learning campus, which had become more common in recent years in European countries, with integrated access and identity across the age range of students, including adults. However as the 'through school' was forming it started to develop these more integrated concepts within the resources it had available. The 'through school' was introduced by New Labour, following research into how children face the leap from primary to secondary school, which showed boys' education in particular falling backwards through this transition period. Since earlier trials with schools that cover the Foundation Years through to Key Stage 4, many schools in England have merged to make this provision, with the Coalition later endorsing this idea, which is now commonly known as the 'all through school'.

The schools that formed an initial partnership in 2003 had retained their individual identities despite sharing a common location. But, in 2007 at the start of the field research, the schools came together to form the 'through school' known as Newtown Federation, inclusive of children aged 3 to 16 years. All three schools had a history of low academic achievement. This can be traced back to 2002, through Ofsted reports and SATs results. The issues of school performance, management, and governance arrangements had become closely interlinked with the Newtown community and its low levels of confidence and aspiration.

This poor performance resulted in the adoption of a new initiative devised by New Labour, which sought to tackle the links between disadvantaged communities and poor educational performance. The Full Service Extended School national pilots aimed to improve pupil achievement by introducing broader services into school and making significant improvements in the home-school relationship (DfES, 2002). As a result the focus on the home–school relationship and the broader needs of the pupils and their families commenced in Newtown prior to the national Extended Schools policy of 2005 and its more radical iterations later on in the Children's Plan (DCSF, 2007a). Newtown's schools became one of these pilots.

Interviews with Newtown's service leaders and practitioners showed that in 2003, when Full Service Extended School piloting commenced, there was low confidence and self-esteem in both staff and pupils, in the three schools. Conversations with parents included accounts of teachers heard 'shouting abruptly at pupils in the grounds of school'. There was a lack of respect for the schools and neighbouring facilities such as the playgroup. Vandalism was rife, leading to a resident commenting: 'that the owner of the glass company was making a fortune as a result of the continual stream of call outs'. Accounts were provided of 'outdoor equipment destroyed by young people on a regular basis' and a 'general lack of respect for the schools'. All three schools suffered falling rolls, but in particular the high school.

The on-site playgroup was the main preschool facility in Newtown. An inspection in 2003 reported that the playgroup provision was 'acceptable overall' and children were making some progress while the schools were judged as 'failing'. In 2008, following the Full Service piloting developments, the inspection of the schools found them 'good in many aspects ... satisfactory in others'. The schools had also progressed towards improved measures of performance. The infant school came out of special measures in 2004 and by 2008 was noted to be 'good with some outstanding areas'. The junior school in 2004 was considered overall 'unsatisfactory', but by 2008 had 'turned around' to be considered 'good'. The high school in 2003 was placed in 'special measures' with comments about 'pupils' attitude and behaviour being unacceptable'. The inspection carried out in 2006 noted a marked improvement in the school with judgements of 'good' and comments about the improved quality of the curriculum and pupils' improved achievement. The 2011 inspection also judged the high school to be 'good' as was the junior school in 2013.

The Full Service Extended School pilot status of the three schools dating back to 2004 had, according to the Community Manager, started to 'blur the distinction between the individual schools and their partners' and 'the Extended Schools policy' published in 2005 'was merely a progression of work already started'. Ofsted considered this broader engagement with pupils and families had helped the schools to improve.

Moving towards Extended Schools

When the research commenced in 2007 the three schools had enjoyed national pilot status as a Full Service Extended School since 2003/4, which formed the basis of their transition to Extended Schools. Indeed they had a head start, due to this piloting activity.

Newtown's approach to the Full Service School

Farrington LA and the three schools' governing bodies commenced the piloting of the Full Service Extended School concept through appointing a new school leader. This new School Improvement Officer challenged the

Newtown: Extended Schools and a community rebuilding itself

schools to start a process of deep engagement with the community, which involved gaining a broader understanding of children and young people that attended these schools. Observations of Extended Schools partnership meetings in 2007 revealed a mature and confident approach to partnership, supported by all three headteachers. The partnership was inclusive of a diverse range of children, young people, and family services from both the voluntary and statutory sectors. However further investigation demonstrated this had not been an easy journey for the schools or community-based staff.

The Full Service Extended School pilot status required comprehensive governance arrangements to be in place to develop the 'opening up of the schools to new partners'. In return it brought additional resources to the schools, primarily in the form of the new senior role of School Improvement Officer, with a school and community background, who was later to be renamed the 'Community Manager'. This less formal title, by which the appointee preferred to be named, 'was far more apt and descriptive of the direction of the role'. However the Community Manager also insisted that all her work 'despite being focused upon the community, was all about school improvement'.

For many years prior to this new pilot, the schools and the wider community had received considerable additional funding linked to the high levels of deprivation in the area. Other communities that were part of this study did not have access to these extensive additional resources. The Community Manager said 'the Full Service Extended School application [had] consisted of four sides of paper', and that she had been the key leader in pulling together local governance and partnership responses, whilst noting that at the same time in 2003/4: 'Headteachers came and went, one lasted six months and another two lasted eight months. Times were difficult but I took up the challenge of setting out a framework and stuck at it.'

A group of interested governors came together from across the schools to support the Community Manager in forming what eventually became the Extended School Board (Table 5.1). Headteachers in 2004 were focused upon 'improving teaching and learning' and largely disregarded the work of this new appointee. However the HMI monitoring visit of the Full Service School provision of 2004 supported this new community engagement, noting: 'how impressive the Community Manager's contribution towards the schools is'. The Community Manager was confident that her approach was the right one to take, despite it challenging the headteachers of the infant, junior and high schools. She also commented upon the first national evaluation of Full Service Schools that implored schools to:

invite people into your school, open your doors and that only [not schools getting out into the community]. I did not agree with this and thought it [the Full Service Extended School] is about recognizing what is out there [in the community] and working together. The principle is two way i.e. community in the school and the school working in the community is also important.

It appeared that not only Newtown but Ofsted and the national government were also learning about how schools could work with the community. The Community Manager discussed her views of engaging with Full Service schooling in terms of the 'social capital brought to the role' and recognizing children are part of families and communities and that 'knowing the community is important'. She thought the strength of the Full Service Extended School policy was its minimal prescription and that it 'provides space to listen to the community and go forward in a flexible way'.

Table 5.1 Newtown Extended Schools Board

Extended Schools Board	This Board commenced as the Full Service School Governors meeting. It developed into the key body to manage and provide direction for Extended Schools and the later development of Newtown Federation
Chair of the meeting:	A nominated governor from a Newtown school
Meeting supported by:	Newtown's Schools Community Manager
Members of Board included:	Interested school governors from across the school governing bodies of the infant, junior and secondary schools

School improvement: Classroom and community

The Community Manager set about developing an annual community survey that 'cuts across the age ranges and gives us evidence of what agencies do, as well as what the community wants'. School staff 'found it difficult to understand', referring to the commencement of engagement with the community, with their view 'that all [their work] must happen at school in the classroom'. This led to 'a presentation to [school] staff about the Full Service School and the Every Child Matters policy, but some only recognized

Newtown: Extended Schools and a community rebuilding itself

it if of use in the classroom'. And, in terms of engaging with the community, 'some school staff do not have a clue about the issues I deal with!'

Whilst the cross-school governors' meeting supported the Community Manager in developing the role, in the first years of establishing the Full Service Extended School the school leadership and teachers remained steadfast in their sole focus upon 'school improvement through classroom practice'. By 2008 the community agenda supported by the emerging broader Extended Schools policy, with its associated joint-working across a range of services, started to change schools' attitude, so that 'Extended Schools are not a bolt-on [to school], they have become part of it' or, as a local resident described it: 'as significantly helping teachers bridge the gap', that had existed between the schools and the community.

New forms of school leadership not readily accepted by the community

At the earliest stages of the research in 2006 it was very clear that the Community Manager was central to the implementation of the Full Service Extended School and its later policy iteration in the form of Extended Schools. There appeared to be no detectable boundary between the Full Service Extended School pilot and the Extended Schools agenda published in 2005. The Community Manager referred to this as 'a natural progression of my work', which provided the three schools with the advantages of understanding each other and their community and the challenges that lay ahead (unlike the schools from Orpintown and Gadley featured in this research).

An Extended Schools Partnership Group (Table 5.2) was established by the Extended Services Board to help it oversee day-to-day development of new services. The chair of this group, a local resident, supported this step in that: 'the benefit is to the community and the school is part of the community'. But in interviews with managers in other community-based services, longstanding mistrust was evident between the schools and other local organizations. A voluntary sector manager was concerned that schools that had suddenly moved into the community and were trying to bring services together after many years, were 'jumping on the bandwagon, which gave rise initially to a strong suspicion about their intent'. Another local voluntary-sector manager, who was trying to make sense of this shift from all three schools (having been for many years inward looking and then starting to engage with community-based services) thought that: 'all teachers are bothered about is teaching children to pass their tests – rather than broader children's development' and this new stance was 'very challenging to community-based organizations'.

The Community Manager was aware of these tensions and worked hard to engage with residents and service managers based in the community whilst at the same time challenging the school culture associated with inward looking performance. 'It is all about interpersonal skills and they have to be finely tuned, with communication a key factor. It is also about keeping your eye on the longer term.' While from school-based staff she was accustomed to 'taking short-term pain for long-term gain'. However by 2009 the headteachers of these local schools talked about their confidence in and praise of the Community Manager, in terms of both the school and the community. One highly experienced headteacher revealed that: 'I have never worked in this way before ... it is a development that underpins everything that goes on really. It took me a while to get my head around it.'

Those working in the community, from part-time nursery assistants through to Farrington's LA councillors, also discussed how they had been involved in a steep learning experience. Schools looking outwardly also changed teaching and learning practice in the classroom. Examples observed included the introduction, for Year 11 pupils, of input from local employers and further and higher education providers, in preparing them for their next steps after statutory schooling; and in the primary sector, parents working with children in the classroom.

As a result of the development of the partnership, a common realization emerged that parental attitudes towards school and young people's aspirations were significant issues in Newtown. About this the Playgroup Manager commented: 'there was a lot of low self-esteem in parents and as a result short courses are now run which make them feel more confident in themselves. So, "yes I can do that" is a phrase we hear, replacing "no I cannot".'

According to a headteacher the merger of the three schools brought about, through the Full Service School pilot and subsequent Extended Schools response, a totally new approach to schooling, alongside the newly developed community work:

> The federation has broadened out our [school] view. Instead of individual children, we talk about families. Whole packages for families, the 13 year old in the high school, the 6 year old in the junior school and the 3 year old in the infant school. We can join up at our review meetings instead of considering individual children, we involve the whole family.

Newtown: Extended Schools and a community rebuilding itself

Table 5.2 Newtown Extended Schools Partnership Group

Extended Schools Partnership Group	This group was initially developed by the Community Manager to work with the community in the development of the Full Service School agenda in 2002. It transformed into the working group that later developed all the Extended Schools provision under the direction of the Extended Schools Board, which moved to an advisory role. The Extended School Partnership later transformed into Newtown's key planning group for community development, inclusive of all the service provision to the estate.
Chair of the meeting:	A local resident and ex-pupil
Meeting supported by:	Newtown's Schools Community Manager
Members of the group included:	Farrington LA Councillors
	A host of voluntary sector services working on the estate covering children, young people, and families. Some with specific functions such as sports development
	Local professional football and rugby clubs
	LA Regeneration Services
	LA Young People's Services
	LA Library Services
	LA Early Years Services
	LA Sports and Leisure Services
	LA Education Welfare Services
	Victim Support
	Police
	Faith groups
	Playgroups
	NHS health service providers

Schools and community-based organizations learning to work together

Observation of local meetings, which brought together programmes for the community, noted how despite the partnership existing for five years, all players were still learning from each other and constantly reflecting about their own and others' roles. The Community Manager was known to be 'very skilled in bid writing' and sourcing money for additional work. Despite this vision and leadership, all individuals' contributions were welcomed and there was joint ownership of new services, examples being the summer play programmes, Easter activities, Christmas fun, and before- and after-school work. A mutual sense of responsibility for the quality of delivery and success of these programmes had developed over time between the 'through school' and approximately 20 community-based organizations. A selection of the very extensive new services, developed through this growth in partnership working, is summarized in Table 5.3.

The Extended Schools Partnership Group meeting drew together funding streams from a range of organizations and members of the local partnership regularly discussed approaches such as 'trying out this' and 'see how this may work'. This reflected openness between the diverse managers and local practitioners who were able to learn from each other. They had drawn a shared conclusion that there were no 'off the peg solutions' to building community engagement and confidence, or to improving standards in the school. An example of this was the holiday scheme that engaged with parents, children from the playgroup, infant, junior and high schools. A comprehensive programme was devised drawing together funding from charities such as Children in Need and Sport England, as well as the LA, police, and national government.

To reach this level of trust took a long time, many years, and involved the pooling of expertise. However, it was the Community Manager who was charged with the responsibility of reporting back to funders for each piece of work and the outcomes associated with it. This was a complex task as funders asked for outcomes related to their own area of interest. The police expected to see a reduction in crime and anti-social behaviour, whilst a sport organization required updates on improved sporting activities on the estate.

A teacher from the infant school noted: 'how the schools were learning to work together as well as with the partnership' and school leaders and visiting Ofsted Inspectors were learning 'to gain an understanding of whole child working'. Towards the end of the research a manager from a local voluntary organization summed up the feeling of local managers and practitioners:

> At the beginning [of the partnership working in 2002] we were conscious about stepping on each other's toes. We now all know what people [services] are doing in the area and we plan accordingly. That is the basis of it [the partnership], to make sure we don't end up with all this duplication and we end up with a fantastic package of resources for the community. That is everybody contributing to it, that everybody gets out of it what they want to and that we are giving the children what they need and want. So everything is feeding back into the group [partnership meeting]. For example children asked for x, y, and z. We could not provide it but can anyone else provide it? It works in that way. It took a while and people are breaking down barriers [between the organizations] and they know that the others in the group are not there to steal their ideas. We get on with it. So that is one of the big outcomes, in that people have lost their fear of working together and now have confidence in each other.

The LA Youth Work Manager, talking about partnership working and the ongoing community surveys to assess local need, added that:

> The Community Manager has brought together agencies. Normally I would have to meet them on a one-to-one basis to review what is going on and come back with some proposals [for youth work in the community]. Now the Community Manager brings everyone together I don't have to do that we [the partnership] know the community needs. So I think this is really fantastic.

LA councillors who joined the group in 2009 were highly impressed with the pooling of resources from over 20 organizations and how, through processes of 'trying things out', they were learning openly about how to work in new ways with the community and the new understandings gained of Newtown. This led them to ask the partnership to become the local regeneration partnership, absorbing within its remit a much wider role of economic regeneration for all residents, a role far exceeding that of the local Extended Schools partnership concerning children, young people and their families. But this attitude was not reflected across all LA services. Headteachers discussed issues related to engaging with Children's Social Care: 'The problems we encounter are with Children's Social Care. They are the same as they were ten years ago. They "close cases" at the drop of a hat and put us as the Lead Professional.'

Table 5.3 Newtown Extended Schools: a selection of services developed

The services developed by Newtown Extended Schools Partnership Group included:
- The facilitation of localized integrated multi-professional working around families – a radical shift in emphasis from crisis intervention associated with Children's Social Care to one of the early intervention and prevention; including support for 'step down' from Children's Social Care interventions into more universal services
- The development of a building on campus into a multi-professional centre for delivery of services and a community learning facility
- Holiday play schemes – covering all holidays including Christmas, Easter, and all half-term holidays
- Before- and after-school clubs – including breakfast and homework clubs
- Family support work
- Developing engaging events with the whole community such as circus skills
- Day trips and residential weekends to provide pupils with new experiences such as theatre or the seaside or countryside and for parents and children to take part in such trips or residential weekends
- Intergenerational activities both formal and informal – such as learning to dance
- Sports events – including links with established professional sporting organizations and the use of their venues
- Safe cycling and broader safety events and training for children and families
- Work with teenage parents
- A diverse range of work around the health agenda with both parents and children
- Victim support – in response to high rates of crime
- Prevention of youth crime and anti-social behaviour
- Diverse range of young people services from youth clubs to individual support programmes
- Playgroups – including targeted support for more vulnerable children
- Crafts and craft fairs
- Support with careers and employment work for both parents and pupils – including formal qualifications

Newtown: Extended Schools and a community rebuilding itself

- Practical courses for parents such as first aid
- Vocational courses for parents – including formal qualifications
- Support in developing a new Children's Centre and all that this provided including a comprehensive library facility
- A range of community events to support the community in building confidence – as requested by the community – particularly in the context of community cohesion

There was a distinct tension between those working in schools and the statutory welfare services and how they related to each other: 'Children's Social Care come in, throw it up in the air a bit and then close the case and walk away from it'.

Similarly residents, though largely recognizing the improvements locally, held a range of views on where developments had got. Some echoed the view of the partnership and the renewed role of the three local schools in the neighbourhood: 'schools are getting better. They listen to us. You can go into school here and ask anything. You just walk in and talk to them.' But some recounted their earlier experiences: 'a lot of teachers talked to parents like they are kids' and others recalled how 'school's work starts and ends at the school gate. It is like a bubble, kids get out in the real world and they do not have a clue.' But overall parents appreciated that now 'we are a lot more involved [in school]' and 'the schools listen to us' compared to when 'the three schools used to be run by a clique of people. But now all three schools are open. The headteachers have an open door policy and you can go to them about anything.'

An analysis of the Newtown experience

When the research commenced Newtown's schools had been moving towards becoming Extended Schools for four years, via the Full Service Extended School piloting activity. There were still many developments to undertake as the schools merged into one 'through school'. The following sections will engage with some of the key themes that emerged from this research.

New Labour experimenting with new approaches to school improvement

Newtown's schools were threatened with closure in 2002 due to longstanding poor performance and falling numbers of pupils on roll. The community was also at a low ebb with high levels of unemployment and crime and low levels of confidence and self-esteem. A picture of the community losing faith in the value of education was coupled to a cross-school response internalizing issues and utilizing 'school improvement strategies' focused upon classroom practice. New Labour was experimenting by developing pilot activity that engaged schools with considerations of children and families broader than that of schooling linked with competition. They appeared to realize that their policy responses in their first term of office, largely based upon school improvement focused upon the classroom, was not producing improvement in school performance in disadvantaged communities. Improving schools in these poorer communities was a stubborn issue and in areas such as Newtown little improvement had been made since 1997. There was a recognition that poverty and low levels of achievement were continuing despite improved resources and investment both in schools and in communities. The Full Service Extended School pilot introduced a new dimension to schooling in Newtown. It brought together New Labour's multiple strands of funding. As we will see, this proved to be a key issue.

New school leadership qualities required and the role of local governors

The Community Manager was new to the schools and brought a deep knowledge of working with families and communities, which instantly questioned the purpose of schooling. Tension between the internalized school improvement agenda and a community-focused agenda occurred in the first years of bringing together schools to work in partnership. Headteachers 'came and went'. Schools were learning about each other as part of developing a mutual approach to the Full Service Extended School, whilst a new front, the community, started to open up to them. The schools' workforce was coming to terms with a new area of work involving much wider considerations than that of the child in the classroom. The workforce, including headteachers, were challenged to gain understandings of education or schooling involving much more than a sole focus on teaching and learning in their own organization, the infant, junior, and secondary schools.

As well as bringing 'huge social capital', as the Community Manager referred to herself, she used the school workforce's lack of understanding of the community to establish her autonomy, initially considering 'the community as my territory'. However she also brought together governors from the three schools to act as a support for this new agenda, and to make decisions about the direction of the Full Service Extended School. These governors were in full support of the Community Manager and recognized that the schools as they were in 2003/4 were unable to effectively engage with children to improve standards, never mind with their parents. The Community Manager had a long-term vision for the community, as the

Newtown: Extended Schools and a community rebuilding itself

Full Service Extended School policy allowed great flexibility and room to manoeuvre. The Playgroup manager and staff were also local residents and could see the direction the Community Manager was taking and provided full support – they also felt, despite being on a school site, that they were alien to the schools.

The first signs of school staff realizing the benefit of the Community Manager's approach was through an HMI visit, which aimed to learn from the Full Service Extended School pilots. This had appreciated the value of the 'community work in terms of school improvement'. However, as the Community Manager stated on several occasions, there was 'short-term pain for longer-term gain' also in terms of the community. After many years of the three schools looking inward, disregarding the community, and of some staff in the high school seemingly in continual conflict with the community, both families and community-based services were very wary about the Community Manager's intentions. Rapid change was on the cards as the direction of Extended Schools started to emerge nationally and play out within Newtown community. To make this situation even more complex, the history of agencies in the community was that of working in isolation from each other. So there was evidence of mistrust and a deep-seated belief in keeping your work to yourself, 'otherwise it may be stolen'. Organizations viewed themselves in competition with each other for 'access to funding streams' and 'positive outcomes'. Although Newtown was able to draw down funding from a variety of sources and had a wealth of organizations working on the estate, historically practice was based upon silo-minded, discrete professional and organizational cultures.

Community-based services and partial understanding of children

When these historical accounts of local service approaches are drawn together it can be concluded that the professional and organizational practice in Newtown involved a partial view or understanding of the child. These partial views were constructed by a range of agencies including regeneration, housing, schooling, youth work, and so on. The success of the Full Service Extended School and the following development of Extended Schools appeared to lie with the Community Manager and her longer-term approach and drive to develop a partnership of schools covering ages 3 to 16 years and linking together disparate services working in isolation in the community. The commitment was to engage meaningfully as a leadership figure with children and families and bring about change for families and the broader community.

This mission rose above the long-held professional and organizational interests and associated practice found in Newtown. The Community Manager understood schooling and communities and engaged with others incrementally so they could appreciate this more complete understanding of the child and their life within the family and community. This was indeed an engagement on three complex fronts to change basic understandings of themselves as managers and practitioners and their perceptions of others alongside this discovery of the child in the broader context. Perhaps this explains the Community Manager's long-term commitment, which took some ten years to achieve and was affirmed by a resident in 2012 stating 'schools are now part of our community'.

The Community Manager alluded to how she went about achieving this mission, saying: 'I take a community development approach', which involved 'getting partners together and is very, very time consuming'. Those taking part were discovering that children and families were central to their work rather than organizational and professional interests. Analysis of data demonstrated the approach involved empowering players through 'an honest dialogue'. The development of the partnership meeting that brought together service representatives was not led or chaired by the Community Manager but chaired by a resident who also worked on the estate. This was a deliberate ploy to engage with the prospective partners on a more level playing field. Developing partnership relations was a drawn-out process involving all partners being valued and considered equal within decision-making processes. A sense of trust was built between the partner organizations across many years leading to a new focus, not upon themselves, their practice or their organizational interest, but as one stated 'we are all dedicated to a child and family focus'.

Despite Extended Schools placing school leadership figures in charge of developing local multi-professional partnership, by 2007 in Newtown there was a sense that all venues were engaged, from the church through to a small playgroup. The Community Manager was building a community plan not merely for pupils and their families, but for the wider community. Thus a further strand emerges in terms of developing a new culture, a new approach to Newtown.

The development of a new mutual localized professionalism

By 2007/8 a common language was being used by almost all staff interviewed whether from school or from the 20 agencies engaged in the Extended Schools Partnership Group. A new professionalism had developed locally, illustrated by a notable concern for working with families as opposed to children or young people or parents only. There was a determination to engage with parents following recognition that raising aspirations was a key issue for all concerned. This was not only about schooling, but about broader areas such as employment or career options, issues through which the community could gain confidence in itself. The playgroup staff encouraged young mothers and fathers to take short courses. The infant school ran a host of daytime courses for parents covering a broad range of areas such as understanding how the school worked, parenting classes and confidence building. The high school ran courses on the school site to engage parents in learning that would benefit them in terms of making choices and engaging in training or employment. Jobs were key to the agenda and conversations with a range of practitioners saw that building parenting capacity and a feeling of being able to work was central to breaking the culture that had seen Newtown's children leaving school with very little in the way of hope.

The opening up of schools to parents and the engagement of parents in children and young people's services in the community provided a vehicle through which the Community Manager could bring multiple cultures together. The schools, as well as delivering the national curriculum and improving the quality of teaching and learning, engaged in gaining broader understandings of their pupils through the opportunities facilitated by the Community Manager, and this approach became recognized in Ofsted and LA reports as centres of engagement for parents. The agenda with the community-based organizations started a long process of merging understandings, practice, and resources as both school and community practitioners provided increasingly seamless provision of new opportunities. The 'through school' lent itself to what headteachers referred to as 'a family approach' as opposed to 'a child centric approach'. Schools were learning about broader services and these services were learning about how schools work and what priorities each had, whilst all could appreciate the difference being made in terms of the community. These improvements included children respecting the school and its equipment, less anti-social behaviour on the streets and a community with a stronger voice and the confidence to talk to services about what they wanted. A worker commented: 'it is no longer our job to tell people what they want. It is for us to deliver what people want.'

This partnership served as a programme of mutual learning or perhaps a more apt word would be discovery, across a complex landscape of schools, broader services and the community itself through which this new local mutual professionalism was forged. Newtown's schools and community-based services during the period 2002 to 2010 received high levels of funding compared to other communities that took part in this study, but the coming together of these organizations, which historically were noted for their hostility towards each other, brought great benefits to the community. A wider understanding of children and families was achieved and also the delivery of better value for money with improved outcomes for families. This helped the community handle the reductions in public spending that were to follow. The Community Manager was key to this development alongside the gaining of mutual trust and understanding between the parties. But it was constantly noted that funders could not cope with this partnership working model. This was apparently due to funders continuing with 'silo' approaches to requests for funding commissions, based on partial considerations of children and parents, as they had not been through the learning processes associated with the partnership.

A key activity throughout the research was partners continually 'trying out' new practice and 'listening' to each other, through which new ideas emerged. This proved to be in effect a synthesis of diverse professional practice, supported by integrating local funding streams through which partners concluded that this way of working could improve the offer for the community. The Community Manager took responsibility for the key action of merging local funding streams and at the end of the 'summer activities programme', for example, she worked to divide the positive outcomes of the programme into the outcomes that funders required or considered as measures of success in relation to their own individual funding streams.

Whilst this new way of working caused the Extended School partnership to evolve through the invitation of local LA councillors into the Newtown Regeneration Partnership covering all aspects of the community, there were tensions between the partnership and some services delivered by the LA and PCT, in that these commissioners did not understand the new mutual working that was being developed locally in Newtown. As the Coalition's decisions to reduce public spending started to impact upon funding available in Newtown, this multi-professional approach to the community softened the blow of potential reductions in provision, due to the effective ways services were working together. However, while organizations such as the police had successfully engaged in the partnership, others such as Children's Social Care had not. So when the research concluded there was still work to do to engage with and more fully develop a holistic response to the community. But perhaps that reflects a key issue that emerged through the research in Newtown, that developing holistic responses to families is a long-term and complex task.

Conclusion

The journey schools, local services, and the community undertook was a long one that involved a leader with a vision for the community. The role of Community Manager was central to developments in terms of the breadth of understanding of schools and communities and the skills brought to a community and its schools, which were faltering. Through a prolonged process of learning about each other, schools and community-based services guided by the Community Manager gained new understandings of children, young people, and Newtown community.

Interventions based upon organizational and professional perspectives and therefore partial understandings of the children and families were contributing to a community with low self-esteem. Bringing together service providers, using the Full Service Extended School pilot which eventually morphed into Extended Schools, saw the gaps between each of them close and new holistic engagements being invented. This was why New Labour set upon this unprescribed policy direction so that flexibility could remain and local partnerships form and work in ways that best responded to each community's need. Through this, schools changed their understanding of children and families and in return became recognized and valued as part of a more confident Newtown community.

Chapter 6

Extended Schools: Contribution to the schooling discourse

Introduction

This chapter will draw out a selection of key areas of learning that emerged from the case-studies covered in the previous four chapters and evaluate how Extended Schools have informed the discourse concerning English schooling. Developing Extended Schools was not a straightforward affair. It involved many complex and interrelated issues that led to fundamental challenges to the professionalism of all concerned. Consequently a diversity of insights materialized from this longitudinal research in four communities, but this chapter will confine itself to three common themes that arose from the case-studies. They concern:

- schools coming together
- schools discovering community-based services
- the forging of a new mutual professionalism based upon new understandings of community.

In essence this involved a process of schools moving from narrow conceptualizations of their pupils to develop broader more mutual understandings with their new-found partners, representing a fundamental shift from a professional focus upon education in its narrower sense towards one of education in its broader sense.

The chapter will then consider if the research fulfilled what it set out to do, followed by a discussion concerning how New Labour's experimentation with the English schooling system has raised some fundamental questions about the nature and purpose of schooling itself. The chapter will conclude by reviewing the conditions that gave these educators a range of choices much wider than those associated with the contemporary debates concerning school performance and governance. Extended Schools provided a brief interlude when educators and their partners were partially freed from the constraints of policy solely developed through a combination of neoliberal and neoconservative approaches. It offers a glimpse into what alternatives for the English schooling system might look like.

Theme 1: Schools coming together

This section examines how schools initially responded to developing local partnerships as they came together in their communities. The first step in the Extended Schools journey was for local schools to gain better understandings of each other. This provided the foundation upon which their local partnership could start to grow.

Differing factors brought schools into a closer local relationship

Developing Extended Schools through the formation of partnerships in Orpintown, Gadley, Hayfield, and Newtown was not a simple case of following the government's policy direction as it emerged from Whitehall. The schools in Farrington LA moved towards the Extended Schools agenda much earlier than the schools in Eastfield LA. Deeper investigation indicates initial moves by Hayfield and Newtown's schools were not linked to the development of national policy on Extended Schools nor was it about Farrington LA promoting schools working together. There were other factors involved.

The introduction of a broader engagement in children's lives in Hayfield commenced through the high school and was instigated by its principal. His early experiences as a school teacher fundamentally influenced his approach to the role of teaching and purpose of schooling. He considered the role of a successful school to be about embracing a broader understanding of pupils and their families than that prevalent in approaches to schooling in the early 2000s. The infant and junior schools in the area also began to consider broader understandings of children than those confined to the classroom. Linked to this shift in the fundamental role of Hayfield's schools was the lack of local services to meet the needs of Hayfield's children. The schools through imaginative deployment of their budgets formed the basis of a multi-professional team upon which local partnership working evolved. New Labour's policy development of Every Child Matters in 2003 and the associated Extended Schools in 2005 acted merely to support the direction of travel of Hayfield's schools.

The schools that serviced Newtown were considered as 'failing' by both Farrington LA and DfES. They were suffering from poor attendance, poor behaviour, low occupancy, and below expected levels of examination results in the context of school league tables. Strong accounts came from all quarters, including the community, that Newtown's schools were considered of little value by a community that had lost confidence in itself.

In 2002 Farrington LA was approached by DfES to establish a national pilot. Following New Labour's election victory in 1997 and a huge investment in education, particularly in inner-city areas, improving SATs results was proving to be difficult in disadvantaged communities. Government response came through the Full Service Extended School pilots, which aimed to improve standards through a much broader approach than that involved in contemporary considerations of school improvement. Three years prior to the first iteration of Extended Schools, the pilot aimed to learn about how schools in disadvantaged areas could improve standards through devising new multi-professional local practice.

Farrington LA was concerned that the schools serving Newtown faced closure and nominated the infant, junior, and secondary school to engage in a new venture. The appointment in Newtown of a senior leadership figure with much broader knowledge and experience of children, young people, and families than that of the school workforce was the first step towards partnership working. This appointment, in 2003, proved critical to introducing a new approach to schooling that involved bringing together Newtown's schools to form a new relationship with the community. As with Hayfield, the New Labour policies that emerged, such as Every Child Matters and Extended Schools, were merely a supportive corroboration that Newtown's schools were moving in the right direction as the Full Service Extended School progressively developed into the Extended School.

Eastfield LA for many years had maintained informal partnerships between schools. It used these existing and what proved to be rather loose partnerships to first instigate localized responses to the Extended Schools policy as it emerged in 2005. Orpintown and Gadley schools were prompted to respond, which triggered the transformation of their informal partnerships into ones with capacity to deliver the Extended Schools Core Offer. Unlike the schools in Newtown or Hayfield, at this time there was little in the way of broader approaches to schooling evident in Eastfield. Gadley's high school immediately grasped the concept and saw Extended Schools as a way to transform their approach to schooling, which had been 'in name only as a community school'. However Orpintown, despite its strong sense of 'town pride' and the high school offering adult education courses and also hosting the local sports centre, appeared slow on the uptake. It failed in its first attempt to bring schools together to develop the Extended Schools Core Offer and seconded a much more senior manager in 2006. It was on 'catch up' when the research began, and under pressure from Eastfield LA to develop a workable local partnership.

Overcoming a culture of schools working in isolation

Though both Eastfield and Farrington LAs claimed to have existing localized school partnerships prior to Extended Schools emerging, they proved to be extremely informal and it was the individual triggers described in the previous section that started meaningful local interschool dialogue.

Orpintown's schools were on the cusp of developing a joint response to children that needed 'time out from formal classes' but the research revealed that, overall, the schools in this community worked exclusively in isolation from each other. Orpintown's primary schools operated within a culture of competition in the local market place for pupils and a consequence of this was they knew very little about each other or how they operated. School leaders appeared to gain peer support from other school leaders sited in more distant places rather than local schools. These supportive relationships were forged where headteachers had been previously employed or where they may have trained together with other colleagues. Locally good practice was not shared, nor were the issues or difficulties individual schools faced discussed at local level. These schools proved to be overwhelmingly inward-looking. This experience was similar in the other partnerships that participated in this research, however in Orpintown's schools these features were more pronounced and regularly verbalized in terms of ongoing tensions between the schools.

Hayfield's schools had started to engage on a mutual journey as far back as 2001 following the high school's lead. But in Gadley, by the time the research commenced the local schools were apparently learning through their early Extended Schools experiences to also form a local overarching Schools' Partnership. This partnership led to closer cooperation across many functions of schooling including the timetable, curriculum, and the production of a local offer to all pupils.

Multiple historic accounts from residents, those working in schools and community-based services noted how the three schools in Newtown, despite all judged as failing around the turn of the millennium, were working in isolation from each other as totally independent units. This occurred despite pupil transition from infant to junior to high school. The Community Manager upon her appointment in 2003 immediately brought together governors from the three schools. These governors supported the idea of Newtown's schools working together to overcome what appeared to be immense issues in relation to both school performance and community confidence.

In these four communities schools initially saw each other as competitors or rivals in a market place for education services. It appeared that some school leaders also thought the Extended Schools agenda was irrelevant to them as they strove to continue improving their school performance through an approach that reflected education in its narrower sense. Bringing these schools together within their shared community prompted them to consider new understandings of themselves as a group of local educators and by so doing to moderate their rivalry for pupil numbers. They learnt that they may have issues in common. However, there was also a clear primary and secondary educator divide identified through this research.

The primary and secondary educator's divide

The high schools in all four research sites took the lead role in developing partnerships. Apparently high schools considered they had a superior capacity and more developed management skills than colleagues in the primary sector. However in each partnership there were tensions arising within the primary sector, whose professionals believed they were already more focused on developing a broader understanding of families and communities, compared to their colleagues in the secondary sector. But a much more pronounced issue emerged: there was not merely a lack of knowledge of each other, but each sector of schooling had developed its own form of professionalism. The primary school workforce engaged with parents in the first years of schooling and delivered a broad curriculum to fulfil the government's testing requirements, whereas high schools were much more enclosed institutions with specialist curriculum staff and pupils engaged in following complex timetables, to achieve the required standards to maintain market position. Parents had little stake in their child's education once they had been absorbed into high schools, with their large numbers of staff teaching children through a diverse subject timetable.

The schools in this research were also largely ignorant of other educational sectors. This included the critical transitions where pupils and their families were expected to confront these distinct forms of professionalism as children progressed from one stage of education into another. Schools were learning about each other as they moved to develop partnerships on which new services could be based and they also discovered that they too had to come to terms with and reconcile the differing professionalism of the educator in the primary and secondary sectors.

School leaders and a workforce professionalism set within a narrow context

Linked to the earlier discussions around differentiated approaches to the engagement with Extended Schools, in terms of both timing and rationale for constructing this agenda, different school leadership approaches also proved to be a key factor influencing how developments played out.

Orpintown's school leaders appeared to be in conflict with each other about how to approach Extended Schooling. A new temporary and relatively junior member of staff in the high school was appointed to lead local development. Some primary school leaders chose to ignore these developments whilst others engaged with them. But as previously discussed those working in the primary sector believed their professionalism and leadership style meant that local partnership working should be led by them. However the research demonstrated these primary educators also had little in the way of understanding or knowledge about the wider community within Orpintown's entire school workforce regardless of the sector. The SEN leader from the high school was perhaps the nearest the local schools had to someone who understood the principles of multi-professional working although this was in the setting of very specialist disability services. She also had some understanding of the gulf between the educational sectors through taking responsibility for SEN transitions across the primary and secondary sectors. This provided her with acceptability to primary colleagues in terms of developing the local partnership despite working almost exclusively within the secondary sector.

But the high school's leadership viewed these new local Extended School developments as being for 'those pupils who did not fit the academic mould'. The school was an excellent and high-performing school and the principal sought to continue this educational business with a focus upon academic qualifications, whilst Extended Schools would offer those 'less successful pupils' a broader offer through new local partnership developments. Perhaps this approach reflected a stage in altering the deep sense of professionalism set within contemporary considerations of 'school success'. This response was an expression of a leadership and professionalism that considered Extended Schools as being an issue largely for 'problem families', despite the 'universal offer'. In the primary sector some players accepted a broader understanding of Extended Schools in terms of universality, but other colleagues ignored the agenda and did not engage until the partnership was well upon its journey.

Once promoted by Eastfield LA, Gadley's leaders saw the potential of Extended Schools and quickly realized their lack of knowledge of the community and that there was an urgent need to appoint a new leader with much broader understandings of children, families, and communities. A secondment opportunity of a youth and community manager filled this role and became the key player in leading the partnership. The skills introduced into the school workforce by this new leadership figure were quickly recognized by Gadley's school leaders in terms of converting the secondment into a permanent senior-leader post within the newly devised mutual schools structure. This Extended Services Manager drove forward developments in a direction that engaged with the leadership of both the primary and secondary sectors.

However there was some questioning about the contribution of schools to partnership developments. A twin track developed when schools were coming together, schools were learning about each other facilitated by the Extended Schools Manager while at the same time she took on the task of developing partnership working with community-based services. This was particularly the case where primary schools initially did not consider Extended Schooling as a priority for them. Gadley's school workforce was in a similar position to Orpintown and extensively questioned the need to 'fritter away the budget' of successful schools on community-based work. The Extended Schools Manager extensively engaged with the school workforce to support their understanding that pupils have lives outside the classroom.

In Farrington LA, the leadership of Hayfield's principal was unique in the context of all school leaders engaged in this research. He was committed to seeing pupils through a much broader lens than that of his contemporary peers. Almost all school leaders were brought up on a diet of school improvement through largely internalized technical processes concerning classroom-based practice. The changes in Hayfield's schools workforce had taken place before the research started and seemed to be largely embedded across the schools. However, the principal discussed how not all the workforce was fully engaged with his views on schooling and some teaching staff might consider engagement with the community as a low priority. A teacher explained how when he came to work at Hayfield he thought he was an experienced teacher who had received excellent 'teacher training'. However his Hayfield experience challenged him to engage with new constructs of children, inclusive of family and community, as opposed to that of the classroom only.

Newtown's school leaders, following the establishment of the Full Service Extended School in 2003, continued with their exclusive fixation on teaching and learning set within technical approaches to classroom practice. These 'headteachers came and went' and each proved to be unsuccessful in their mission to improve standards. This provided the Community Manager with the freedom to work in Newtown supported by school governors from the infant, junior, and high school, who believed that community engagement was the way to improve standards. As with Gadley a new leader was required who had a much broader professionalism than that of the existing school leadership. The Community Manager considered pupils in the context of the family and community whilst other school leaders largely saw pupils through the lens of teaching practice in the classroom.

Like Gadley there appeared to be a dual track taken in Newtown consisting of the Community Manager developing work with community-based services, while engaging with the school workforce to try to 'change hearts and minds'. The Community Manager had to prove to these school leaders that there were alternatives to school improvement focused solely upon classroom practice. This led to conflict between the Community Manager and the school workforce. Teachers could not understand why Newtown's schools should engage with the community. They reflected the narrow approach to school improvement of their school leaders and a compliance with the traditions associated with it. Changing the schools' leadership approaches and workforce professionalism took many years to achieve. It was HMI visits and Ofsted's recognition of the Community Manager's approach that started to change Newtown's school workforce considerations of their pupils, accompanied by a growing realization that standards were improving through community engagement.

A key issue that emerges from comparison of these first initial steps to draw together responses to the Extended Schools agenda was that of the leadership and professionalism of the school workforce. Both had become positioned within what appears as a partial understanding of children and young people, with its emphasis on a concept of schooling that involves schools being judged by narrow indicators concerning an educational agenda set within a regime of school performance and the traditions that go with it. The schools that took part in this research had been working since 1988 as autonomous bodies in a pseudo-market dominated by school league-table positions based upon examination results, inspection reports, parental choice, and increasing central government control. School leaders had been encouraged by successive central governments, both Conservative and New Labour administrations, to develop this approach based upon schools in a competitive market place. The development of Extended Schools, other than in Hayfield, exposed the narrowness of leadership and workforce professionalism of the schools involved.

Schools coming together: A summary
Schools coming together in their community proved to be the foundation upon which a broader approach to children, young people, and families could develop. The schools that took part in this research were initially working in isolation from each other, with a leadership and workforce professionalism cast within the narrow confines of judgements of 'school success' and a distinct primary and secondary educator divide. This approach reflected the theme of schooling within a framework of education in its narrower sense. Schools needed to introduce new leaders with much broader understandings of children and young people than those in the existing school workforce.

Different triggers started this process of schools coming together. LA pressure to develop a response to Extended Schools was the key through which Orpintown engaged; Gadley's principal and the high school's governing body could see the opportunities the Extended Schools policy could open up to schools; Hayfield's principal held the view that schools should have a wider role than narrow schooling; and Newtown's schools were facing closure due to poor measures of performativity and adopting a broader school role provided an opportunity to save themselves from closure. It was not a case of simply following government policy. In each community school leaders and their workforce were discovering new understandings of their pupils, which marked the start of constructing a new, broader school professionalism, effectively opening up educators to understandings of education in its broader sense.

Theme 2: Schools discovering the community and its services

Turning to the second theme and what could be considered the second phase of Extended Schools development: as schools started to realize that they knew very little about each other, they also began to notice that they knew very little about community-based services and the community itself in which they operated.

Getting out there and learning
In each of the four communities, whatever the trigger may have been to commence the journey, starting to collect information about their

communities and the services available to their pupils and families was the next vital step in developing Extended Schools. Gadley and Newtown's leadership chose to 'buy in' new staff with this community-based capital, Hayfield's principal felt he was able to lead developments using practice based upon a broad approach to schooling, and Orpintown deployed a highly experienced SEN school leader who was used to school-based specialist multi-agency working. School leaders and staff were familiar with some of the services external to their school, such as those that might support children with disabilities; but there was a more complex world outside the school gates.

Following the first failed attempt, Orpintown's schools focused upon existing church-led research conducted within a relatively disadvantaged community. This acted as a platform through which the Extended Schools Manager could engage with community-based services with some sense of understanding using base-line information gathered from Redbury.

Gadley's new leader in Extended Schools knew the community well and the challenge for her was reversed when compared to other managers developing Extended Schools. For her it was to gain understandings of the school's workforce, the primary and secondary school culture, their professionalism and to introduce this workforce to the community, through which they could discover a much broader professionalism.

Hayfield's school leaders were unique in that they had been progressively engaging with 'the broader needs of families', which they understood to be acting as 'real barriers to learning', with little in the way of local services to overcome these barriers. Theirs was a story of inventing new services largely through the imaginative use of school budgets and charitable funds, as they sought to design new resources to address these barriers to learning.

Newtown's Community Manager set a course that seemed initially to bypass the school workforce and engaged with the community and the numerous community-based services, to start to construct new understandings of children contextualized within the family and community. Evidence included 'the annual community audit' that later became recognized by Newtown's school leaders as they realized the limits to improving standards through classroom practice. The research demonstrated, like the observation of Newtown's Community Manager, that this was not a one-way journey 'for schools to throw open their doors to the community'. But this was indeed a two-way process involving school staff working in the community and the community being invited into the school. It was a journey that involved 'getting out there and building new relationships' and gaining understanding of those who worked with the same children and young people in the community. Engagement with Newtown's school workforce waited until there was evidence that working with the community could indeed improve school standards.

Community-based services challenged to work with schools
In Orpintown, Gadley, and Newtown, though much less in Hayfield, community-based services such as local voluntary sector organizations had grown accustomed to their local schools being 'inward looking'. These services considered local schools to be 'insular' and 'self-interested organizations'. They viewed schools as organizations 'out for themselves' and with 'school success', in terms of exam results and associated league tables, as central to their aims. Community-based workers talked of not seeing local schools working in the community for many years. Then schools appeared to not just start to engage with the community but also to insist on leading local developments, despite an apparent lack of understanding of the community. The community-based school nurse through her health promotion role tried to engage with Gadley high school on a broader agenda of sexual health and provided an example of being refused permission to park the health mobile bus on the high school's car park as this 'may give the wrong impression of the school'. There were similar occurrences in Newtown where a multitude of community-based services considered schools as self-interested and they had to be won over by the Community Manager on behalf of local schools.

As schools knew little about others in the community, conversely community-based services seemingly did not understand the mysterious world of schooling children. These community-based organizations, like the school workforce, were working with partial understandings of children and families. But within these partnerships, community-based services knew very little about each other. Sometimes there were multiple interventions that took place with the same families and services were not aware of each other's work. In some cases there were individual children within the family that multiple services worked with, and these services were disconnected from each other. This became evident as schools and their new found community-based partners came together.

Developing new local governance arrangements
School leaders, in particular the high schools' leadership team, dominated local developments in each of the four research sites. Orpintown's school leaders succeeded in maintaining total control of the Extended

Schools agenda through devising a school-led governance arrangement with a consistent though implicit goal of developing responses for 'those academically less able pupils'. Orpintown's school leaders, whilst expecting community-based services to contribute both to the universal and targeted elements of the Extended Schools Core Offer, did not feel that these partners should have voting rights in deciding the direction of the partnership.

In Gadley, the honed community skills of the Extended Schools Manager were the conduit through which new governance arrangements were constructed. But this manager required anyone who joined the partnership 'to bring something [resources] with them to the table [partnership]'. Gadley was also simultaneously developing the larger Schools' Trust and, following their experiences with Eastfield LA, the high school leaders were very concerned that it did not create a local trust with an overly bureaucratic approach to local partnership. The construction of inclusive governance arrangements resulted from the Extended Schools Manager's knowledge and understanding of community work. In Gadley each partner that contributed to Extended Schools had equal voting rights. They marked their inclusive approach through nominating a LA manager from Children's Social Care to chair the Extended Schools partnership meetings.

Newtown's Community Manager took a long-term approach and like Gadley's Extended Schools Manager knew community organizations well. Using her expertise and community-based autonomy, she devised with these services comprehensive and inclusive governance arrangements over a ten year period. But what was different at Newtown compared to other partnerships was the inclusion of school governors from the three schools. This move provided a support mechanism for the Community Manager, particularly as headteachers seemed to wholly focus upon technical classroom practices and any hostilities that arose with the school workforce. It also gave credibility to the Extended Schools Partnership Group through school governor support to manage the Extended Schools developments both strategically and on the ground in the first years of development. These school governors were much more in tune with the Community Manager and what may bring about improvements for both pupils and their families when compared to headteachers and school staff that continued to focus on narrow conceptualizations of education, through which they hoped to improve standards.

Hayfield's Extended Schools developments were supported by a local Breakfast Business Meeting, which took place at least once per term. There seemed to be less need to establish formal governance arrangements as the schools had few local partners due to the overall affluence of the area, which attracted little in the way of community-based services. And what services were there had been progressively engaged with over a number of years. Perhaps most importantly, Extended Schools were nothing new in Hayfield. They were considered day-to-day work and not an additional government policy to engage with afresh.

Schools discovering the community and its services: A summary
Other than Hayfield's schools, which were inspired to move to broader understandings of the community at an earlier date, the remainder of the schools that took part in this research were largely unaware of both community-based services and the community itself in which the schools were sited. They felt a need to get out there and learn about these services and they often found these services also working with their pupils outside of the school environment. Schools utilized different approaches with some 'buying in' highly skilled staff with existing community knowledge. They started to construct governance arrangements with which they could manage the new processes being developed and relationships being formed with these newly discovered partners. These community-based organizations had been working in the community without engagement with schools and these agencies were now challenged to work with seemingly inward looking schools on a new community-based agenda.

Like the triggers for schools coming together, different rationales and a spectrum of approaches were adopted. The schools in each of the four research sites constructed different approaches to Extended Schools, effectively different ways of understanding education in its broader sense. Newtown developed a very broad and inclusive partnership; Orpintown formed a partnership based upon those perceived as less successful pupils; Gadley's partnership had started to replace the local miner's welfare as central to its community; and Hayfield created a host of new local services mainly through schools working together.

Theme 3: Schools and community-based services developing new forms of mutual professionalism
The third and final key theme to emerge from this research concerned a lengthy process of constructing new mutual understandings of children, young people and families, set within the community. This formed the third phase of developing Extended Schools and the professionalism that was emerging reflected education in its broadest sense. But it took many years

to develop what was a local mutual professionalism and it proved to be an ongoing journey for all.

Realizing partial understandings of children

These case-studies illustrated how school leaders and their workforce had mostly embraced a culture that regarded school success as synonymous with narrow performance measures, an approach that ignored or downplayed major aspects of children's development and childhood itself.

The principal had led the local developments that embraced broad, holistic considerations of children in Hayfield's schools before this research commenced. As a consequence when the Every Child Matters agenda emerged in 2003 Hayfield's schools were well prepared and had a good understanding of a broader agenda in relation to children's lives outside school. But, analysis of the data generated from this longitudinal study into partnership developments showed that changing the deep-seated school professionalism elsewhere was not an easy task. Orpintown's schools failed on the first occasion to develop a response to Extended Schools and they learnt that they required a respected and highly skilled leader to start to embrace wider understandings than those they had been preoccupied with. But their perspective was set within a frame of 'those less able pupils' and 'problem families'. However by 2013 Orpintown had moved to embrace a broader understanding of their pupils and for that matter what Extended Schools could offer.

Gadley's school leaders and their workforce realized their shortfalls summarized as being a 'community school in name only'. By 2011 the Extended Schools Manager had succeeded in her mission to widen schools' understanding of their pupils. A similar form of dual process was adopted at Newtown where HMI visits and Ofsted's comments contributed to shifting the thinking of the three school leaders and their workforce to realize that perhaps their understanding of pupils was restricted. Broader realizations that children's lives involved much more than the classroom were in 2011 marked by the principal of Newtown Federation announcing: 'we are now a true community school'.

The previous theme also touched on the issue of community-based services being confronted by schools starting to work in what was seen as these services' territory, the community. They reacted strongly to this invasion as schools became interested in what they had been delivering for many years without interference. Community-based services realized they also knew little about the schooling of children and they were also, like schools of which they were very critical, seemingly viewing children through a partial understanding based upon their organizational and/or professional perspective. Once discovered, schools leaders, their workforce and community-based services started to address this key issue.

Extended Schools: A platform for engaging in mutual learning

Orpintown's Extended Schools Board, as noted earlier, was school dominated in its engagement with the construction of new ways of working. There was conflict at strategic level as headteachers and senior Children's Social Care managers came together to discuss children at risk. Accounts told of the differing understandings of these children at risk and the differing ways schools and Children's Social Care went about addressing the issues. But the real work of developing Extended Schools in Orpintown lay with the two meetings at lower level in the hierarchy chaired by the Extended Schools Manager. The universal services meeting was the first time schools and community-based practitioners had come together to discuss Orpintown's service provision for children, young people, and families. Observation of these meetings and listening to views of the participants revealed a progressive learning experience was taking place. Ideas were being tested out, differing service approaches discussed, and these participants started to construct a new local Core Offer as a result of the learning taking place. There were no quick or ready-made solutions, it took a great deal of time for mutual understandings to emerge from these meetings.

A similar process was taking place in the meetings orientated to more targeted service responses to individual families. Initially these meetings focused upon children who were considered to be experiencing poorer educational outcomes due to their family life. Each party to these meetings was being put in a position of engaging with other practitioners' perspectives on the same child that they were working with. Through this coming together these professionals started to discover preventative solutions to the issues families faced instead of, as they previously had done, waiting for families to fall into crisis. Participating in both of these meetings involved a steep learning curve for all, including the Extended Schools Manager.

Observations of Gadley's meetings pointed to the same inter-professional learning taking place. The Extended Schools Manager understood a great deal about community and the work that took place within it and had to focus upon learning the schools' perspective. Partnership meetings took place less frequently, compared to Orpintown and Newtown, but new localized services emerged from these meetings, in particular new family support services.

Hayfield schools were well along their journey in 2007 as this research commenced. They had already created a school-based multi-professional team. This team noted regularly their frustration with broader LA and NHS services as nothing appeared to be changing locally in these organizations. As a consequence Hayfield's school leadership continued to add to their service provision as they invented local responses to the needs of their pupils. It was later on this journey that Farrington LA realized what the Hayfield partnership was doing and started to use their expertise more broadly across the LA.

Agencies working in Newtown exceeded 20 in number plus three schools, in a so called 'failing community with failing schools'. They demonstrated throughout this research the depth and extent of learning from each other, commencing in 2003, that was necessary to gain a fuller understanding of children and young people. But as the research finished participants noted how they were still learning from each other, though by this time trust had grown to the point that an observer might draw the conclusion that all participants were working for one organization despite their differing organizational and professional labels.

Newtown's Community Manager supported the school workforce and community-based services in recognizing their lack of understanding of each other, and of how they worked with the same families with little knowledge of each other's interventions other than when families fell into severe crisis. Ideas and approaches were continually being exchanged over a ten-year period in meetings whilst developing local plans and undertaking programme evaluations. New localized practice and new services were being constructed as a result of these new mutual understandings. Like schools in competition with each other the services based on Newtown estate felt they had also been in competition with each other, historically. By 2013 the Extended Schools Partnership Group had transformed into the meeting place where all community planning took place. Children were no longer viewed as the property of the school or community-based services, as these services had considered them when they were acting as isolated units. A professionalism that viewed children partially through professional and/or organizational interest was now replaced by broader understanding of individual children set within the context of their whole lives.

In each of the partnerships partial understandings were changing over time and giving way to new holistic understandings of children framed within family and community. These new constructs emerged at different points along the Extended Schools journey influenced by numerous factors and marked with visible signs of changing professionalism. Central to this professionalism were these multi-professional mutual understandings of children and young people.

New localized mutual professionalism and conflict with centralized bureaucracies

As each of the four partnerships formed new mutual understandings it became apparent that strategic managers in bureaucracies that exercised control over services, such as Farrington and Eastfield LAs and the NHS, had not engaged in or been exposed to similar learning. Conflict arose as these local partnerships started to understand more deeply their community and identify local need and different ways of approaching it. Some Extended Schools leaders commented how whilst they were taking part in huge transformations locally; nothing seemed to change in terms of what all called centralized working, meaning particularly their LA.

In Newtown the Community Manager and the Extended Schools Partnership Group were receiving funding in small packages from a variety of commissioners that reflected commissioners' priorities in specific interest areas or outcomes. These commissioners continued to commission silo or separate service provision and the outcomes they required were associated with single elements, e.g. improve participation in sport. After five years of developments in Newtown, these diverse individual funding streams were being packaged or integrated into local multi-professional or partnership formats so that a comprehensive programme was available to the community. But to do so meant the Community Manager was required to disaggregate each programme into outcome measures that satisfied individual funder's specific outcomes. In Hayfield the multi-professional team considered nothing at all had changed as regards Farrington LA's approach and headteachers described how this held back local integrated working.

Some of Gadley's practitioners, such as the Youth Services Manager, were able to manipulate Extended Schools to achieve better outcomes in terms of the Eastfield LA's targets. Other practitioners described how Eastfield LA and NHS commissioners and planners were out of synchronization with what locally were viewed as radical changes in service provision. In Orpintown raw conflict was experienced between headteachers and Children's Social Care managers but also PCT and NHS staff were supposedly 'not allowed to engage with Extended Schools as this was not recognized by commissioners'. However, these NHS staff did engage and could see if New Labour's policy direction continued that perhaps schools may be running or managing all services in Orpintown eventually.

The research suggested that local partnerships were gaining new, deep and mutual understandings of their communities through development of partnership working. This resulted in transformational change but managers and commissioners in LAs and the PCT/NHS retained their partial view on children, set within their own professional or organizational interests.

Mutual localized understandings override Coalition policy preferences

The Coalition came to power in 2010 and set about a radical change in its approach to schooling through implementation of an ambitious academy and free school programme. In terms of broader policy the Every Child Matters and the Extended Schools Core Offer became at best optional or at worst disregarded. Schools were directed by the new Secretary of State for Education to return to a focus upon 'traditional educational values'. But despite this sudden change in policy direction at national level, all four partnerships continued to develop their work in the same way, albeit through slightly adapting their language. Over a relatively long period of time in the context of contemporary policy development and implementation, school leaders and community-based staff had constructed strong mutual understandings of ways of delivering localized working. These new understandings appeared to take precedence over the new policy direction of the Coalition government.

The schools in Gadley adopted the government's preferred academy status but practice in the community stayed the same. The Extended Schools Manager placed a new accent on this work, Extended Schools should significantly contribute to improvements in examination results, which appeared to be the central thrust of Coalition school reform. And this Extended Schools approach and the manager's expertise became available through academization to other academy schools in England. In Orpintown the high school, which continued to lead Extended Schools, changed from an LA school to an academy but the partnership remained strong as did the mutual work. A headteacher from one of Orpintown's LA schools discussed in 2013 how schools remained working in cooperation and that mutualism overrode the new national drive towards renewed local school competition. The Newtown partnership continued to thrive under the Coalition, as did the community, as a result of these new ways of working. A similar story was told by school leaders in Hayfield that 'Every Child Matters is the right thing for Hayfield despite being unfashionable with the Coalition'.

Farrington and Eastfield LAs were heavily influenced by their capacity to deliver services as public spending reductions impacted between

2010 and 2014. A consequence of these reductions was that both LAs changed their stance towards Extended Schools development as did some NHS senior managers. Conversations with those continuing to develop Extended Schools revealed how these 'centralized attitudes were rapidly changing'. Hayfield's approach led to Farrington LA awarding the principal leadership of a 'failing inner city school' and other responsibilities for wider engagement in delivering services across the entire LA. In Newtown all Farrington's services were now delivered through the Extended Schools Partnership Group, which had been transformed into the local regeneration and community planning group.

Eastfield LA had been progressively working to develop a model that placed Extended Schools as a vehicle contributing towards the delivery of many of its key services. It appeared that Eastfield LA had come to recognize and value the new localized forms of working that had been developed and the new professionalism associated with this. Perhaps at a time of austerity in public spending this new mutual form of professionalism was also influencing LA and NHS leaders' ways of working.

Schools and community-based services developing new forms of professionalism: A summary

New mutual understandings of children, young people and families were being constructed as a result of building localized partnerships through the implementation of Extended Schools. School leaders and their workforce and those working in community-based services began to realize that they had been working with partial understandings of children. These understandings were framed by a combination of organizational demands and professional traditions. Those employed by schools, LAs, the NHS, and community-based services were subject to the measures of success linked to their organization. Within these organizations deep-rooted traditions had become embedded within each individual professional role. The process of bringing together schools and community-based services provided a platform through which mutual learning took place that challenged these organizational demands and professional traditions, resulting in the construction of new mutual ways of working. A new localized, mutual professionalism was constructed to support local transformational change. But as local partnerships became increasingly confident in what they were developing, conflict arose with leaders working in LAs and the NHS, as they were not privileged to have taken part in a similar journey. Centralized organizations remained fixated upon control through processes such as commissioning that reflected sectoral priorities and long-held traditions.

When the Coalition came to power, with a renewed emphasis on traditional educational values, a strong performativity agenda and increasingly centralized control of schooling, accompanied by ignoring policies that were central to local transformational change and localized mutual professionalism, these partnerships continued to take the same direction, albeit that language was modified to fit with this new national agenda. The Coalition visualized successful schooling as education in its narrower sense while the schools that took part in this research continued to view education within it broader sense. They had learnt it was 'the right thing to do' and the Extended Schools journey continued.

Some key lessons for the research

This research aimed to understand how schools and community-based services were responding to New Labour's Extended Schools policy by gaining insights into the impact the policy had upon school leaders and their workforce and those working in community-based organizations, and how their approaches to children and families changed. It has shown how Extended Schools challenged all that were touched by the policy. School leaders, the school workforce and community-based services were given permission and freedom to work together to form local partnerships and they were expected to engage with their community in new multi-professional ways based upon Every Child Matters principles. More specifically, the research has shown that:

- Policy development was not always the trigger for transformational service change. Hayfield's principal considered the English schooling system as too narrow and before the advent of the Every Child Matters or Extended Schools policies, schools had commenced an ambitious project to place themselves at the heart of the community. But others such as Orpintown's leaders were content with being appraised as very good schools in terms of performativity, despite a realization that some children were not achieving their full potential through present ways of working.
- Schools were working in isolation from each other despite being in the same community. These leaders and each school's workforce were set within a professionalism fostered by the market place that viewed neighbouring schools as competitors.
- While there appeared to be a shared professionalism among school leaders and the teaching profession, there were at least two distinct and clearly defined cultures within the schooling sector: primary and

- secondary. These divided educational sectors needed to be reconciled prior to local Extended Schools partnerships being built.
- There were exceptions to these different school professionalisms. Hayfield's school leaders and workforces had adapted to understand broader approaches to children, families, and the community.
- Schools described a partial professional view of their pupils set by a framework formed through the school performativity lens and the traditions associated with schooling, although again Hayfield proved to be an exception to this finding. Similarly community-based services knew little about the processes of schooling children in their neighbourhoods despite working with the same children; they also knew little about each other and their interventions with the same children. It was concluded that these community-based leaders and professionals also worked with a partial view of children engaging with their services.
- All, other than Hayfield, were challenged by their engagement with Extended Schools (and in Newtown with the Full Service Extended School pilot in 2003) to start a new dialogue between leaders and professionals working in the same community. A learning process emerged that played out at different levels among leaders and front-line staff. This learning took place between schools, between schools and community-based services and between different community-based services.
- Within the space provided by Extended Schools for these new local conversations between different interest groups, alongside the discovery of these partial views, a new form of local mutual professionalism was starting to be constructed. Newtown demonstrated that it took many years to develop a localized mutual professionalism. The time taken to gain these new understandings reflected the depth and intensity of the partial constructs of children held by almost all leaders and professionals who participated in the research.
- Developing new understandings was not an easy process and a spectrum of responses developed out of this work. These responses included initial hostility between schools, between schools and community-based services, and between community-based services themselves and at times the community itself.
- Local partnerships represented the first steps in moving towards local transformational change as tangible new local partnership structures emerged. The Hayfield partnership took the lead, eventually placing

schools as central to the community via the construction of a new Community Forum that engaged in a diversity of issues. In Newtown the Extended Schools partnership transformed into a community forum, which embraced comprehensive service planning for the area. Gadley's initially small venture fostered the development of a trust that eventually led the development and management of a number of academy schools, and through this the local Extended Schools learning was transmitted to other areas of the country. And of more significance locally, Gadley's schools and their broader engagement with the community quickly filled the vacuum left by the loss of the coal mining industry. Orpintown drew together schools, community-based services and the town council to foster a new local spirit and 'town pride'.

- These partnership structures took different forms and developed at different times but all provided an opportunity through which to engage with the community.
- Those schools that opted to join the race towards academization, including some of those schools that led Extended Schools developments, also retained their multi-professional localized working, although it was noted that the language changed to better suit the Coalition's standards agenda.
- The new local voices generated by this partnership working in communities led to conflict being played out over a number of years between LA and NHS managers and these new partnership leaders. The 'town hall plans' such as the LA Children's Plan were being challenged by new localized iterations of community need. It took several years before Eastfield and Farrington LAs started to recognize these new local plans and in some cases promoted these partnerships as places where their services could be delivered.
- In the communities themselves, despite the complexity of issues that confronted leaders and practitioners, there were noticeable changes to how services were working with residents. Residents talked of schools opening up to the community and becoming interested in much broader issues than when they were considered inward-looking and self-interested organizations. Schools were repositioning themselves as central to the community, framed within a new localized mutual professionalism.
- When the Coalition came to power in 2010 they disregarded Every Child Matters and the associated Extended Schools agenda, describing them as a distraction from a refreshed policy agenda based on schools in

competition with each other. Schools were asked by central government to return to so-called 'traditional educational values'. Whilst DfE took direct control of schools that converted to academies, including some schools leading Extended Schools in this research, all four partnerships continued broadly with the same trajectory, informed by the learning that emerged through Extended Schools engagement.

This research was fortunate to take place at a time and in places where radical localized transformational programmes were emerging. It was set within an environment where the 'rule books' appeared to have been thrown away or, perhaps better described, with hindsight, suspended. Schools and community-based services were inventing their future by learning from each other and testing out ideas. Deep insights were gained into how schools and community-based services responded to these freedoms provided by Extended Schools. As the research was being written up in 2014, engagement with the partnerships demonstrated that leaders had started to move on, through retirement and promotion, yet strong traces remained of Extended Schools.

But there was some anxiety that the loss of interest in local multi-professional working nationally inevitably would erode the drive and commitment of these local leaders as the Coalition chose to continue to ignore these partnerships' contribution to children's and families' lives. And with a General Election on the horizon and the potential for further policy shifts there was also an increased sense of uncertainty amongst members of the partnerships. But there was also a view that emphasized the need for further local integration of services as LAs became increasingly influenced by financial reductions in budgets with Farrington reporting a 40 per cent loss of their total budget since 2010.

The educator at the crossroads

The research revealed that the introduction of New Labour's Extended Schools policy started to raise fundamental questions about how schools and community-based services worked within these four communities. These educators implementing Extended Schools learnt that they were essentially at a crossroads and choices lay ahead of them. Whether it was through voluntary decisions such as at Hayfield or a shift in approaches through being mandated such as in Newtown and Orpintown, starting this new form of engagement or experimentation opened up both schools and community-based services to new challenges. This experimentation in schooling was devised by New Labour and formed part of a new approach to service provision they named 'progressive universalism' (Cummings *et al.*, 2011). This research provides a glimpse into the alternatives that lay outside the dominant neoliberal policy approach, which had by the millennium permeated all the services that took part in this research and was accompanied by neoconservative traditions, particularly within the schooling sector.

We saw that services working in these communities displayed a range of differing professionalisms, set within different traditions, and moulded most recently through the application of neoliberalism based upon target setting and competition. Simple short-term measures of success for schools prevailed and the position was similar in those services that started to interact with these schools. Schooling under New Labour remained largely in competition, a marketized public service approach inherited from previous Conservative governments.

Children and families had become 'service users' and organizations were also held to account for their success or failure through simple measures. Fashionable terms frequently used by services such as 'partnership', 'collaboration' and 'multi-agency working' appeared to be largely illusory as leaders and their workforce worked within a mindset of childhood framed by these simple organizational measures, linked to partial perspectives or views of children limited and characterized by the drive for success.

At first glance Extended Schools seemed quite an insignificant policy (Cummings *et al.*, 2011). However, its implementation saw the professionalism of school leaders and their workforce severely challenged and led to new understandings of what schools might be like. Extended Schools started to provide educators with new freedoms. These educators were asked to lead the construction of new local ways of working with community-based services. While continuing with the school performance agenda they were granted the challenge of engaging with others to construct local multi-professional partnership approaches in the community. The eight-year span of this research witnessed radical shifts in professionalism, the first few steps towards revealing alternative approaches.

School leaders understood there was more to children's lives than being pupils in the classroom and community-based services started to better understand local schooling, both realizing that there was much more than 'performance', whether as a school or as an individual service. Participants were incrementally discovering that there were different ways of working than those engrained within their existing, frequently silo-based professionalisms, fostered by organizational interest. Hence, the educators who contributed to this research found themselves at a crossroads, having been drawn into a notably quiet local revolution. This was a revolution that seemed somehow under the radar of many policy commentators and academics, not to mention the general public (as also the whole Every Child Matters policy agenda had minimal public recognition). While New Labour apparently continued with policy with inherent neoliberal and neoconservative traits, they seemed also to be shifting away from a market-orientated approach to experiment with a new agenda that placed leaders and practitioners at a crossroads.

A reanalysis of data in 2014 provides understandings into the conditions, that is the type of environment, these school leaders and community-based services found themselves operating within that supported the construction of new, seemingly radical local alternative ways of working.

Extended Schools creating new conditions and different choices for the educator

Interviews with national policy makers and New Labour's Children's Ministers revealed how schooling and children's services were being subject to policy experimentation that sought to bring about social change as the market on its own could not be trusted to provide solutions to fulfil their social justice ambitions. It therefore would seem important to understand the conditions that supported this experimentation to be undertaken at community level by school leaders and their partners. The following themes emerged from the reanalysis of data.

Local approaches and flexibility

All four case-studies illustrated how developing a local partnership was an important factor in supporting the transformational journey towards mutual working. The Extended Schools policy provided the freedom for schools to lead change at very local level. But even at community level, the journey would prove to be a complex one. Should central government have pitched these transformational approaches at higher level such as LA level, as they had done with the Every Child Matters policy in 2003, the journeys would have been far too complex taking account of the higher level geographical issues. Local engagement between those who took part in Extended Schools, coupled with the other factors listed below, provided a supportive environment in which transformational change could take place, and some new models could emerge from which others could learn. Therefore the issue is one of geography and flexibility that supported the development of a new professionalism.

No assumptions
Linked to the above issue of local approaches, or localism as it is often now called, we saw that each group of local schools in 2005 was at different starting points in working towards these mutually constructed partnerships. There were no assumptions made within the Extended Schools policy of schools' positioning in 2005 in relation to the community and existing working practices. Schools, as the research has demonstrated, were positioned on a spectrum of engagement with the community. Some in 2005 were engaged with the community whilst others were not. Extended Schools policy made no assumptions as to the starting points of schools on this partnership journey or their positioning with the local community.

No prescribed processes
Central government policy production has a tendency to be accompanied with prescribed process models. A review of policy history demonstrates this is particularly evident when policy is concerned with transformational change. Extended Schools did not involve the application of set processes or procedures or route maps as to how best progress local developments. Whilst DfES provided limited examples such as those for governance structures to help local partnerships, these were only possible aids. In this research partnerships developed their own individual local governance structures and planning frameworks around local conditions.

Minimal measures of success
Implicit within almost all government policy development are expectations of what success looks like and the how success is to be judged. This is usually laid down in government documentation using terms such as 'milestones'. School leaders supported by LAs were expected to develop Extended Schools over the period 2005 to 2010. The Core Offer was the indication of success but this offer was flexible and to be designed around local factors. The Extended Services Core Offer (DfES, 2005) comprised: a menu of activities, including study support and homework clubs, sport, music, arts and special interest clubs, combined with formal, 'wraparound' childcare in primary schools; parenting and family support, including family learning; swift and easy access to targeted and specialist services (for example, speech and language therapy, behaviour support); and (if appropriate) community access to school facilities such as sports grounds, ICT, and adult and family learning. We can see this offer had a great deal of flexibility within it.

No prescribed outcomes

New Labour aimed to produce local partnerships that would reduce educational disadvantage and also provide localized conduits through which the flagship Every Child Matters policy could be implemented. However in terms of prescribed outcomes for children and young people, whilst school performance measures remained in place, there were no preset requirements with the Extended Schools policy as regards outcomes for children, young people or families, unlike almost all other New Labour's policies: examples include the number of teenage pregnancies or reductions in young people offending or incidents of anti-social behaviour. Extended Schools partnerships were able to develop their own local plans and local measures of success.

No outside influencers

Central to Extended Schools developments were the bringing together of services in local communities with schools. There were no experts in this field to advise or prescribe how to successfully develop these local partnerships. The research did not unearth any outside experts to interfere in the process of building local partnership development, whether this be outside consultants, governmental organizations, LAs, or academics. Developing Extended Schools was a new organic experience that involved local leaders and the workforce, devoid of any external influencers. Those usually considered as 'experts' were in fact on 'catch-up', as these local partnerships led transformational change. The National College for School Leadership was an example of a leading schools organization on 'catch-up'. Their publications were learning from local partnerships about new school leadership approaches, from those set within a market-led approach to ones exploring a wider, more creative community-based approach. These organizations were learning from partnerships, as this new role for school leaders was set in uncharted territory. Developing Extended Schools in these four partnerships was an incremental and organic process based upon reaching local mutual understandings, unfettered by outside influencers.

Trust and freedom to design the future

Finally in terms of the conditions that allowed these local partnerships to thrive outside the dominant performance culture were the issues of freedom and trust that replaced the market and tendencies towards central government control. Through research interviews with two national policy leaders and two former Children's Ministers, all of whom were key agents of this policy development, it became evident that New Labour was engaging in experimentation. This was an experiment that could lead to a radically different construction of state schooling and the services that support families.

Like their Conservative predecessors, New Labour was well versed in setting prescribed solutions within a competitive market. But in this case they decided to launch schools on a journey that went outside the current convention of market solutions. Central government knew the market was not working for disadvantaged children in school, so whilst they held schools to account for performativity, they also provided unprecedented freedom for them to experiment: to search for and discover new solutions to an intergenerational issue that historically had reduced opportunities for children from disadvantaged communities, compared with children from wealthier communities. These local developments aimed to provide insights into how to tackle deep-seated structural social issues. New Labour asked schools to provide answers to questions they themselves could not answer. They trusted local leaders with this policy development.

Perhaps this is the most important condition that enabled an environment to be created that fostered cooperation, trust, and mutuality, resulting in new mutual forms of multi-professionalism to develop. Those delivering services were trusted to construct solutions to the issues individual children face, both in terms of educational achievement and the broader areas of their lives.

Returning to the theme of the educator at the crossroads, the positioning of schools and community-based services and their development of a localized, mutual professionalism poses an interesting question. What might these partnerships look like in 2030, should the Extended Schools policy continue to be supported by successive national governments? The next chapter, through applying the conditions that support the development of this new type of professionalism, will envisage what schools might look like if Extended Schools had continued to be promoted by central government.

Chapter 7
Looking ahead: The school in 2030

The final contribution this work will make to the discourse on English schooling, having set out in the previous chapter the position of the educator at a crossroads, is to develop a vision for future schooling through application of the understandings that resulted from this research. This account of what schools may look like in 2030, some 15 years after the conclusion of the original research, is constructed through the utilization of the conditions in which these original pioneers of Extended Schools found themselves working. New Labour policy provided hints that the dominant discourse surrounding English schools, of performance and governance linked to deeply engrained neoliberalism and neoconservativism, could be questioned and that there are indeed possibilities beyond present conceptualizations of schooling.

This research suggests that educators and schooling were at a crossroads in 2015 and so a further research visit is made to one of these four Extended Schools partnerships, 15 years into the future, the year 2030, with the intention of understanding what might be found.

Preparing for the research visit to the partnership in 2030 I engaged with the internet to see where the partnership I selected might be. This took some time, the schools that made up the partnership I last contacted in 2015 no longer existed and that schooling was now an integral part of the community, via the Community Campus. The familiar characteristics of neoliberalism that I had become used to engaging with, that framed schooling within the simplistic performance information used by parents, through which they made choices about schools, were not available on this website, nor were they available through the national government's website. There was nothing about school league tables or Ofsted reports. After reading through the website I was confused, so I adopted my trusted methodology and asked to start this round of research by undertaking a short observational site visit and a research interview with the school leader. This may help in understanding this seemingly unfamiliar territory. In fact, there was no headteacher or school principal, but there was a Campus Facilitator who, via an online appointment system, I arranged to meet.

Upon approaching the community there were signs directing me to many different community facilities. I asked a passer-by where the campus was, to which they replied: which site did I want? She said that the community and the campus facilities were interwoven and therefore there were several sites. I asked for the administrative site where the Campus Facilitator might be and was directed accordingly. Upon arriving at my destination I noted that I had indeed passed other campus facilities and there seemed to be a network of cycle paths connecting them and a small bus station outside the entrance of what seemed the hub or main facility. The bus station was being used by children and adults, connecting to other communities and through to the city centre.

The older mix of 1930s to 1970s school buildings and temporary classrooms had gone and been replaced by new buildings spread across a purpose built campus site. These buildings appeared to be designed with sustainability in mind and looked very different to the schools in which I researched. There were many open spaces with gardens and cafes. The school fences had gone, as well as the gates. Playing fields were integrated into what appeared to be a local public park with retired people playing bowls and others exercising dogs. I also saw groups of children and adults using these open spaces and wondered if this was part of schooling in 2030. This campus was really not a campus in the sense that I knew it, that is a separate educational campus such as those often found in the higher education sector, but a collection of buildings interwoven with the community itself and apparently central to the community's life. This reminded me of the local approaches towards integration offered through the original Extended Schools policy.

I was greeted at reception and asked for the Campus Facilitator. A young man, that I later learnt was taking a higher education course in business management, escorted me to the Campus Facilitator's office. On the way we discussed how this campus when considered with its network of distributed facilities is the largest piece of public infrastructure in the community and a central focus for not just students and pupils, but for all residents. We also discussed how higher education students had recently moved into the area from another campus to undertake the same business management degree modules and had been given accommodation in a campus building with other higher education students. It became quickly evident that this work placement on campus was the first work experience on this student's course. The course was held on site and further business-based placements were providing students with the skills and competences and experiences through which to apply the theoretical approaches linked to higher education. Employment was high on the campus agenda, with local businesses connected to an onsite employment centre. This student talked of also volunteering with young people in the community to support both young people's and his own personal development. He said that the campus was focused upon education, but this covered a wide range of areas from health through to housing and financial advice and from early years to further and higher education. This seemed on first sight to be an all-encompassing, mutual, community-orientated place. Extended Schools had developed to a point that passed my expectations by far.

We passed a number of small business start-up units in the enterprise area next to eating and leisure areas. There were children and adults of working age mixing in these areas with older retired people. By now my understanding of the English schooling system was severely challenged, and I felt ill-equipped to engage in research in this seemingly alien environment. But, I reflected upon the important condition New Labour had applied in 2005 of making no assumptions as to the positioning of schools and their relationship with their community. Things had certainly moved on since my research concluded.

An electronic pass system was in place. People were wearing some sort of small device that allowed free access from one section of the campus to another. I had noticed local residents outside the facilities also wearing these, so it suggested to me that these devices were widely available to members of the community. As well as fairly traditional looking lecture spaces, there were lots of other spaces where children and adults were working together. I was looking for the usual hints – the teacher talking to pupils from the desk sited at the front of the classroom, a central feature of education since Victorian times; the name badges denoting individual professional roles and indeed ranks, but I could not see any of these recognizable traditions. I also looked for the clues as to which organizations were working on the campus. Neither were any organizations identifiable nor were their names on the office doors to help me understand the types of services offered here. Young children were playing in what looked like Early Years settings and young people were working with tablets in rooms and appeared to be debating issues. But perhaps these young people were not pupils, as there were no school uniforms worn. There were small theatres and arts areas, some with musical instruments and lots of electronic equipment. Then I noticed an art installation. A sign informed me that it was work from a community summer-holiday programme. But of concern to me were the lack of computer classrooms, or books in these rooms, or even a library.

A noticeable common link came to me, that children and adults had small tablet devices with them as they walked around the campus. Perhaps paperless learning had arrived and information technology was the means to support exchanges of knowledge and information outside that of human interaction?

Upon entering an office I was introduced to the Campus Facilitator. By this time I was extremely confused by what I had seen and was questioning myself about what I should ask in order to understand what had transpired in the 15 years since last visiting the Extended Schools partnership. I thanked the student for guiding me through this new world and after exchanging pleasantries and signing the usual research ethical agreement, I got on with the task of interviewing the Campus Facilitator.

The Campus Facilitator explained that she was employed by the city authority but was wholly accountable to the community through a local board. Using her tablet, she projected upon the wall a number of diagrams, which showed the relationship between her and other organizations that joined together to form this integrated local facility. There was a clear accountability between these organizations (which were locally managed, voluntary sector in nature, I learnt later), the community, and the city authority.

It seemed as though schooling, as well as being linked closely with broader services, was now sited within a space governed through locally-constructed democratic processes that worked at differing levels. At a city-region level there was an overall accountability for all the campus provision, like this one I was visiting, as this was the source of the funding – so familiar. The city-region elected representatives also coordinated regional functions such as communications, including roads, transport services, and supplies such as power and water. But more importantly I learnt that the local campus and its network of facilities were wholly accountable to local residents, including children and young people. This accountability was for all aspects of its development and covered the employment of the campus staff that were on the City authority's payroll. There were structures through which local residents, again inclusive of children and young people, were elected to serve on the local board of the Campus. These residents were accountable to the community, through regular engagement, for the management and direction taken in developing the Campus. Further diagrams showed how the Campus had been developed and built in phases following the learning gained from the early Extended Schools partnership. However, over 15 years and with an increasingly sceptical view of 'top down' democratic processes, a position had been reached through which new localized democratic processes had grown via the development of accountability. This campus was truly under the control of local residents. At first sight it seemed that schooling was now strongly linked to a new form of local democracy, not central government as it was in 2015.

The Campus Facilitator explained her role and that of all those involved in the venture, its aspirations and how these community aspirations could be supported. The campus was inclusive, not just for parents and children as I recalled seeing in my earlier research, but a facility for all. By 2018 the idea that central government and then in turn local government could dictate how educational opportunities should be delivered in this community were over, as was a belief in quasi-market forces to act to improve standards. Similarly the notion of educational traditions such as those linked to elite schooling no longer existed. In fact the English schooling system as I knew it on my last visit had also gone. A crisis had occurred nationally with school places in 2017. Central government had not taken account of the population growth and linked to the fragmentation of the schooling system through academization, lost track of the number of school places needed. In effect, due to the lack of places, this issue caused schools to become the consumer, selecting children who fitted their performance agenda while many children were left with makeshift temporary schooling. This rework of market roles contributed to public dissatisfaction with the competitive schooling system. Now in 2030 education was central to society and democracy.

The Community Facilitator re-emphasized that the campus was about inclusive education for all and not merely about schooling children, as I had inferred. National government produced a framework within which education was developed in the context of lifelong learning at differing levels, from early through to higher education. But at community level, through this localism agenda, tailored perspectives were designed into the range of educational resources available. The Extended School partnership had also concluded, following pressure from the community, that the days of professionals working independently from each other and their associated fragmented views of children and families and the community were over. A new mutual professionalism had grown and each practitioner had learnt to respect others' roles, which greatly simplified understandings of and interactions with the community. The community was now central to the planning and delivery of all services. This included what I had known to be community-based services in the original study and these, alongside schooling, had become further integrated within the community itself.

Professional mutualism, grown through a policy with no prescribed processes or measures of success, had also overcome the remnants of competition in the system. The evidence had been presented to both central and local government that this mutual professionalism provided the freedom to place children as central to their work and radical improvements had been demonstrated in terms of 'traditional educational measures', but in particular for disadvantaged children, their families and the community where they lived. I thought of the work of Anning *et al.* (2006) and Frost (2005) and of the partial understandings of children and the failures of public services to not always protect children from harm. And that the investigations almost always revealed poor information sharing across professional and organizational boundaries. Both central and local government had gained trust in this localized, flexible model originating from the Extended Schools policy, as opposed to the alternative of marketization and its seeming failures. Local professionals integrated together and started to work for the community instead of a maze of different organizations with different approaches, vested interests and different markers of success. The community knew much better than government what they wanted from the educator and how to make professionals work for them. The days of the outside influencer, with a range of theory and policy most frequently based upon deficit assumption of communities they knew little about, had gone. Children were no longer 'tagged' with labels such as SEN or in need of special identification such as with the 'Pupil Premium' of the 2015 era. These historical approaches had deployed deficit modelling to assess what the 'problem is' or 'problems are'. Thinking had long passed this point and each child, like their adult counterpart, was now considered an individual with relationships with other children, their family, and community. And most importantly, someone to be listened to as opposed to an object to which to apply prescribed processes and measures of success. It was not just that the buildings making up the schools I had researched were gone, but the understanding and conceptual framework of what school is was rebuilt, alongside the construction of this campus and its network of facilities.

The Campus Facilitator explained how this site was known as 'the hub' and that the other sites I had passed by in the community were all linked to it. She spoke of these hubs in each community across the city as being configured in different ways around community issues and priorities. The key drivers were each community's relationships with these new types of educators whose role was to guide and facilitate developments on each campus. So each hub and its smaller sites took different forms with different approaches and were staffed in different ways. She also explained that the site covered what I knew as early years, primary and secondary education, adult education, and further and higher education; all were integral to the campus and its wider network. But these labels had long since been dropped and education was now considered a continuum for all from birth to adulthood. It seemed as though the community and the people that served them were indeed trusted to design their own future.

I rather naively asked about competition between this campus and its network components within the community, to which the reply was 'why should there be competition with other community facilities?' These were the traditions that were central to schooling since the late 1980s, so I asked a further question concerning competition between different communities and their respective campus provision. Was one campus considered better or higher quality than the other? Again the reply consisted of a question. Why should we conceive the educator, the facilities they use, and the community to be in competition with other educators facilities and communities? It seemed that the neoliberal and neoconservative approaches as described by Apple (2001) that had dominated my practice were now discredited ideologies and no longer considered of value in terms of educating children or adults or the provision of broader services for families.

Major market failure, which rather echoed that of the 2008 recession, had brought into question the approaches that had dominated the last quarter of the last century and the first two decades of the twenty-first century. Recurrent market failures were also accompanied by growing alarm with the impact of global warming, which was attributed as the cause of several serious environmental disasters around the world. A combination of incidents had led to a fundamental distrust in central government, the markets they fostered and were in thrall to, and the associated philosophy that had become central to western societies.

The new localized mutual professionalism that had grown out of Extended Schools developments created a new relationship with the community and when combined with a new governmental focus on localism, cooperation, and democratic experimentation, fostered the emergence of new democratic processes where the community was now central to practice and not any form of competition or the historical traditions associated with it. It seemed as though education in its narrower sense critiqued by Moss and Haydon (2008) was now obsolete.

The Campus Facilitator went on to discuss how education was now inclusive of wider welfare services. Distinct concepts of 'education' and 'welfare' were now redundant as these different perspectives merged in 2018 as part of the progression of the Extended Schools partnerships. The campus provided these broader services around individual engagement, which was reminiscent of the idea of New Labour's 'progressive universalism' coined in the early 2000s and central to both the Every Child Matters policy and Extended Schools, as a localized platform through which the government aimed to deliver services in a new way. I reflected that this seemed to be what briefly was referred to as 'education in its broader sense' and encompassed considerations of all aspects of children and family lives and the community itself.

The Campus Facilitator listed a selection of services that were available, such as health, financial support, and housing. These services were no longer branded with the names of organizations and the campus had been designed with spaces that dismissed earlier deficit modelling of families and fragmented childhood based on professional and organizational 'silo mentalities'. I considered briefly how professionals talked in the original research about the 'hard to reach' and 'troubled families', but now these concepts of families and individuals were firmly rejected as outmoded. The combination of neoliberal and neoconservative approaches needed branding, traditional forms of professional working, inter-service rivalry and competition, short-term service commissions accompanied by simple outcomes to foster a market, through which to calculate success or failure and the labelling of children through a multitude of assessments that resulted in professionals owning children and the outcomes they, the professionals produced.

The Campus Facilitator went on to support my reflection by explaining that Extended Schools and the new professionalism constructed and its success in engaging with families, particularly in inner-city areas, had discredited these outmoded models. Services were now personalized and yet contextualized by recognizing the interrelationship between children, families and the wider community. This approach reminded me of a school leader's comments from 2008 that 'children don't just bring their brains to school' and how 'they bring lots of complex issues with them'.

The Campus Facilitator discussed how local residents could access high-quality personal healthcare and that health was now totally interlinked with social care, housing and employment and financial support. Apparently other services included social-care workers, probation officers, mental-health staff, psychologists, early-years staff, youth workers, and family workers, as I would know them, although these terms had changed to suit the new [to me] culture of mutual professionalism.

Upon concluding the interview we went to visit some of these campus facilities and this was extended at my request to two further network sites. Again I noted that there were no badges worn and in discussions with staff I met little in the way of issues associated with professional or organizational interests. Staff explained how they engaged with each other on an equal footing using a team approach to provide support for the child or family. What I had known as the school teacher working within the classroom was now part of the team working with children and families. There appeared to be none of the historical hints of professional or organizational hierarchies or their associated ownerships of attachments to children. A sense of mutual professionalism prevailed and the lead professional was said to be whoever was best placed to support that child at that point in their lives; again an echo from the early 2000 era and the policy development that perhaps laid the footings for this campus. The child and family led the approach so had a view of who was best equipped to lead their team. I considered how, historically, instead of working for our own professional gain or that of our organization, the child was the important person and the shared mutual professionalism meant all involved received job satisfaction whoever the main player may be.

But, before moving on to visit a primary learning space, I voiced some concerns with this approach with the Campus Facilitator. Firstly what about the safeguarding of children? This had reached yet another crescendo in 2014 as my original research was concluding concerning so called 'national celebrities'. Children are listened to more intently now was the reply. We take things children say seriously as we do their agency and investigate fully through shared approaches should these types of concerns arise. Children's Social Care is no longer viewed as a separate intervention, it is now part of our integrated approach and as such does not present as the crisis point it used to. The early intervention approach and much better understanding of children, within a holistic approach, had overtaken the considerations of social work as a profession that policed families in crises.

My second question involved understanding what measures of success meant in this new multi-professional world? I was reassured that the culture and traditions associated with the old measures had long gone along with 'silo working'. The new culture involved joint work so that children or adults reach the level of learning they each aspire to and that energies are no longer wasted on chasing targets or outdoing other professionals in competition. These resources are now focused solely upon the individual. Our mutual professionalism far outstrips the success of the old, discredited competitive system and the traditions that went with that. All the work is set within this culture of mutual professional accountability to the child, family and the community and was managed by the community through their democratically elected board. We have gained a new sense of trust both with families and with the bureaucracies that judged us in the past. I was reassured by the Campus Facilitator offering, using depersonalized electronic files, to demonstrate the impact that this way of working was having in terms of individuals who were highly likely to have been historically 'written off' by me or my peers at the turn of the millennium.

My third and final question on this first visit was around the issue of more specialist services children and families may wish to access. Could the campus and its network of facilities provide these? Apparently there were extremely specialist services, an example being, in the health area for children, paediatric oncologists. This was a reminder of the Extended Schools Core Offer and its element of 'swift and effective referral'. And, in the area of higher education, a student may wish to access a specialist course, and again referral mechanisms were in place through which this could be achieved. The Campus Facilitator stated that the campus did not seek to provide all services from cradle to grave. That would be impossible, but at a national level, with the support available through other community hubs, there were collaborative processes developed through which to access specialist facilities. This campus provides an integrated service of the essentials such as education that residents could access locally. But services not available on campus or in its network of facilities were made available elsewhere through local collaborative partnership arrangements.

A further issue was raised by this response, about these campuses being rather like islands of independent local interests. The Campus Facilitator recognized this criticism and discussed the interrelationships between local communities and the influence of global dynamics. A shared understanding had emerged that all communities impact upon each other and a cross-community sense of mutuality and cooperation had replaced rivalry and inter-community competition. While each campus held its own identity, which was extremely important to the community, there were collaborative networks across the UK and using digital technology, an everyday essential of life in 2030, these communities cooperated with each other. This meant that learning and the development of new ideas and knowledge were shared with similarly designed campuses around the world. Education and the mutual professionalism had started to transcend local and national ownership. Education was no longer a commodity to be bought and sold but a matter that concerned global ownership and as such was an investment for all our futures, through European and global networks.

Our conversation continued as we moved from these services to visit a 'learning space', or what I would know as a school classroom. But there was little in the way of signs that this was a classroom, such as a teacher's desk, nor were the tables and chairs facing forward towards the teacher. There were several interactive wall mounted boards and not one as I recalled controlled by the school teacher for the set lesson. Children were clustered in small groups with adults. The children varied in age. The idea of schooling based purely on age and year groups were no longer current. Children and adults were working together on a range of activities. Some were working on interactive white boards, others drawing on large pieces of paper on the floor, and others constructing objects using what I assumed were computers of some kind. There was a buzz in the air as these children were learning through activities apparently constructed by themselves through negotiation with the staff.

I tried but could not discern who the teacher was, or for that matter the classroom assistant (should there still be this role) or the volunteer adult. I did not wish to show my ignorance by asking such basic questions but I felt I should. Apparently these adults consisted of a primary level teacher, a pre-school teacher, an artist, and an engineer, and this activity was a science project about understanding materials and their structural properties. Despite my original research experiences and the insights those Extended Schools pioneers had provided for me into these new ways of working, my thinking about the role of adults within the classroom remained institutionalized. This was team working – the days of the individual class teacher had gone.

The Campus Facilitator, upon leaving the learning space, explained how there were many differing types of learning spaces around the campus. The one I visited was a generic space and used by a wide range of educators and there were more specialist learning spaces for technology and the arts, however time on the visit was limited. Following the discussion in the learning space, I enquired how these professionals were trained in 2030. There had obviously been a huge shift in professional and organizational culture since 2015. I considered how, historically, professional training was mainly delivered by further and higher education establishments and focused almost exclusively upon individual professions, their traditions and approaches to understanding what individual professional success looked like, perhaps as a primary school teacher or a social worker. The Campus Facilitator explained that professional training had lagged behind the development of this mutual professionalism until central government trusted the campus models that were being developed would deliver what they, and more importantly local communities wanted. Those who sought a career in any service were now required to engage in a foundation of common training that engaged with deep understanding of childhood, families, and communities.

Prospective professionals then elect, following successful completion of the foundation programme, to undertake additional intensive training in more specialist roles. However, the mutual professionalism strand ran throughout this second phase of training so that these more specialist professionals understood and could work with a wide spectrum of professionals in a team. These further and higher education establishments had become embedded within the national network of campuses, and their business functions and competitive elements, as with schools, were no longer drivers in terms of success. These student professionals were educated within the range of local campuses through which theory and research could be grounded with their multi-professional experiences in the community. This approach represented an entirely different way of working to my own professional training and a great deal of work had gone into developing a new professional architecture around these new, mutual ways of working.

My visit now extended to two smaller network sites of this main Campus that rather reflected similar experiences to those I had seen on the main campus. A different approach, which was based upon residents' aspirations and delivered through team working, was central to my observations of these smaller sites. The further visits helped with understanding the integrated nature of these public spaces and public services within the community, and importantly not all services were levered into one single large site but these opportunities were available around the wider community.

The Campus Facilitator then escorted me back to the reception of the main campus site as she talked of the great strides that had taken place in the last 15 years since the older, fragmented service modelling, judged by simple measures set by national government, had been finally eradicated.

The educator, a general word that covered this new mutual professionalism, was now trusted to work with and for children and families and not held to account in terms of simplistic measures linked to organizational or professional interest. She talked of how following the capping of funding for both education and welfare services in 2016, this approach had proven to be more efficient and effective in the context of the range of public service models debated by central government over the last 20 years. But most importantly the holistic responses set within a positive educational framework now provided children and families with opportunities they could not have dreamed of when schools and services were fragmented, insular organizations. And this new mutual professionalism had fostered a rekindling of democracy at community level, which in turn caused schooling (as I had known it) to become inexorably linked with the community and democracy itself.

After leaving the campus reception I visited one of the on-site cafés and replicated the approach of my original research by talking to local residents with the aim to better understand the issues raised on my visit. An elderly woman discussed how life had changed in this community. To some extent I could empathize with her view that the changes to schools and welfare services had been rather radical and confusing. However since I last visited this community in 2015, I could understand why this person felt life had also improved and how all residents now exercised an increased stake in their future. She talked of how her friends now participated in this new form of local democracy, where their voices were not just heard but were acted upon. It provided the community with a new confidence, of which the campus was an expression and it reminded me of the first steps I had witnessed at Newtown.

Further conversations in the café with adults of working age, who were also parents of children presently being educated on the campus, revealed they too had a shared sense of ownership of the facilities and the wider community, as did their children. These parents considered themselves part of a local approach to education, both within its inclusive experiences and through localized decision making, set within a fresh approach to democracy. These parents were aware through their own childhood of the historic role of schooling and the myriad of professionals that had worked within their communities in a disconnected manner. They preferred the campus approach, which drew together the capital of a diverse range of professionals but with a central focus remaining the children and families rather than the endless ad hoc, fragmented interventions of their childhood.

Looking ahead: The school in 2030

They described how children automatically enrolled in the campus and when I asked if one campus could be better or provide higher quality education than another I found my question dismissed, in that all campuses engaged with their community to deliver outstanding education and nothing less was acceptable to parents or the wider community. The days of children choosing the best school were over. Parents stated as I left that it is every child's fundamental right to engage with the best possible education and they talked of the morality of the previous nature of education, with a market where there are winners in terms of quality and but also children who too frequently could become losers. One parent exclaimed: 'and losers for the rest of their lives'.

Upon that note I left the campus and reflected upon New Labour's Extended Schools experiment, which I had researched between 2006 and 2014: how it had allowed school leaders and those working in the community to learn and develop better understanding of each other, the children and families they worked with and the community in which they were based. This brief interlude of freedom from an approach fuelled by a combination of neoliberal and neoconservative dogma provided a glimpse as to what might be the role of the educator. I surmised that policy writers, leadership figures, and professionals had been deeply conditioned to work within a framework of competition and its associated traditions and how central government in the last quarter of the twentieth century and the first two decades of the twenty-first century had constructed an environment through which they could increasingly gain control of education and educators. The market and the professional traditions associated with it served to construct a false and fragmented view of childhood. I thought about the research participants who developed Extended Schools and how they were pioneers, searching to discover different ways of engaging with each other as professionals and with children, families, and their community. They took the first few steps towards developing a localized mutual professionalism and provided us with a glimpse into alternative forms of working.

The educator, like our society, is situated at a crossroads signalled by the growing gap between the wealthy and powerful and the rest of us. This trend is also linked to a growing dissatisfaction with our present democratic processes. We can continue on the pathway constructed by a combination of neoliberal pseudo-markets in education and wider services. And as we know all markets involve winners and losers. The increasing centralized control of schooling delivered through the application of neoconservative traditions, serves to alienate growing sections of our society. So my question is a fairly simple one. Dare we consider what we are conditioned to think is the unthinkable? These pioneers engaged with Extended Schools between 2006 and 2014 and showed there are alternatives. Let's build upon the knowledge and understandings we have inherited from them, so that all children have a better opportunity to fulfil their hopes and dreams.

Appendix 1
National policy publications and local partnership developments in relation to Extended Schools development in England

1999	Schools Plus report (DfEE)
2000	National Strategy for Neighbourhood Renewal, linked to Schools Plus (spirit of joining up services)
2002	Extended Schools: providing opportunities for all (DfES)
2002	New Labour articulate the approach on Progressive Universalism
2002/3	DfES considers piloting activity – Full Service Extended Schools (one per local authority)
2003	Government announces the Every Child Matters policy
2003	Newtown Schools commence first steps towards becoming a Full Service School
2003	DfES Demonstration Study in Extended Schools – limited pilot activity
2004	Every Child Matters passed into statue – 2004 Children Act
2004	Schools and General Practitioners, two universal services not required to engage with LA on developing the Every Child Matters agenda outside the issues of child protection
2004	LAs to lead local Change for Children programmes, signalling an enhancement of LA role and responsibility for enacting the 2004 Children Act
2005	DfES releases Extended Schools policy and commences defining the 'Core Offer'
2006	All schools required to engage with local Core Offer by 2010

Appendix 1

2006	2006 Childcare Act, linked to Extended Schools Core Offer – Children's Minister clarifies Core Offer and sets targets for schools
2007	National Children's Plan – twenty-first-century school
2007	Interview with DCSF national policy maker, re potential directions for Extended Schools
2008	DCSF clarification and guidance on twenty-first-century school
2008	Children's Trusts: Statutory Guidance on interagency cooperation. Schools required to work with LAs, signalling a renewed relationship between schools and their local LA
2010	National Conference Extended Schooling – policy drive continues by New Labour and DCSF to continue with twenty-first-century school, schools as hub of services in community
2010	Children's Minister announces schools reach target of delivering Extended Schools Core Offer
2010	Government changes to Conservative and Liberal Democrat Coalition – DCSF to DfE – a refocusing of schools on 'traditional educational values', governance and performance
2010	Every Child Matters policy disregarded although 2004 Children Act remains on the statute
2010	Secretary of State for Education asks schools to focus upon teaching and learning and to disregard broader agendas set by New Labour
2010	Announcement of free school and academy programmes for high schools, followed later by options for primary schools to convert to academy status
2010	Schools considering their position in relation to governance, academic status, and relationship with LA and local partnership
2010	Ofsted refocus on standards agenda leading to loss of Every Child Matters to Ofsted framework
2011	Abandonment of the concept of a national children's workforce and accompanied planning as carried out by the Children's Workforce Development Council
2011	Research interview with national policy maker – recount New Labour policy progression and where next for Extended Schools and multi-professional working
2012	Research interviews with two former New Labour Children's Ministers, to gain understandings into the policy development agenda from Every Child Matters through the twenty-first-century school
2012	Semi-structured interviews with two former Children's Ministers

Appendix 1

2013 Present and former Coalition Children's Ministers approached for research interviews in relation to contemporary policy approach to children, young people, and families and present status of Extended Schools – interviews denied on both occasions

2014 Phase two of research concludes

2014 Further analysis of data from phases one and two and write-up

Appendix 2
Key developments in Extended Schools at local partnership level

2002	Hayfield High School starts to consider embracing broader engagement with community than that of mainstream schooling framed within the performance agenda
2003	Newtown Schools commence first steps towards becoming a Full Service Extended School through DfES and Farrington LA
2003	Hayfield Schools commence the building of the multi-professional team
2003	Appointment of Newtown's School Improvement Officer later known as the Community Manager – commencement of Full Service Extended School pilot
2004	Newtown – three schools set up a cross-school governors meeting to manage and provide leadership for the Full Service Extended Schools pilot
2004	Newtown's Community Manager starts the first of an annual audit of services working in the community and processes through which to engage the community in methods of understanding what the community wishes to see from the Full Service Extended School
2005	Newtown Community Manager establishes meeting of local service managers to commence developing local partnership arrangements and new local services such as summer play schemes
2005	Gadley High School principal raises Extended Schools policy with governing body and with Senior Leadership Team
2005	Senior Youth and Community Manager seconded to become Gadley's Extended Schools Manager, to lead developments of Extended Schools as part of the Senior Leadership Team of the high school
2005	Orpintown High School employs an Extended Schools Manager (leaves shortly after commencing work)

Appendix 2

2006	The field work for this longitudinal research commences – establishing of agreements with Orpintown, Gadley, Newtown, and Hayfield in phases over the next four years
	Data collection methods include documentary analysis, semi-structured interviews, observation of meetings, research diary, and focus groups (with residents and parents in local communities)
	Participants at community level include councillors, LA managers, leaders of services, middle managers, front-line staff – from schools, police, youth service, early years services, private sector, local and national voluntary organizations, the NHS, housing, welfare benefits. A range of local residents, many of them parents
2006	Newtown Community Manager commences drawing down external funding to build new programmes linked to the Core Offer
2006	Orpintown – Extended Schools developments put on hold locally
2007	Gadley Schools commence discussions to seek cooperation and collaboration between them on a much wider agenda than the Core Offer
2007	Gadley commence a process of auditing services in their community
2007	Gadley establish Extended Schools governance arrangements and cross-agency meetings
2007	Hayfield commence formalizing wider community engagement through the development of the Breakfast Business meetings with local service leaders and broader community representatives
2007	Orpintown pressure from LA to restart Extended Services development
2008	Orpintown – secondment of high school member of leadership team to Extended Schools Manager
2008	Orpintown – commence community audit of services and build upon church-led community research
2008	Orpintown develop Extended Schools governance arrangements and establish partnership meeting plus universal and targeted subgroup meetings – start developing the Core Offer
2008	Newtown infant, junior, and high – transition into 'through school' commences for ages 3 to 16 years – DCSF approval of plans to merge schools
2009	Hayfield extend multi-professional team further

Appendix 2

2009	Hayfield commence planning to develop a redundant local sports centre into a community business
2010	Hayfield commence work on developing a community farm
2010	First phase of research written up
2011	Orpintown's Extended Schools Manager leaves – new appointment at SLT level to high school – high school continues to lead Extended Schools locally
2011	Hayfield high school take over the ownership and running of an inner city school and start to apply Extended Schools learning to inner city partnership
2011	Research interview with national policy maker – recount New Labour policy progression and where next for Extended Schools and multi-professional working
2011	Gadley Schools change from Foundation to academy status
2011	Gadley Partnership Trust starts to convert status to become host body for further academies across England
2011	Orpintown High School moves to academy status
2011	Newtown's Community Manager leaves and a new Community Manager takes position
2012	Gadley's assistant principal becomes a National Leader in Education and starts to advise academies on developing Extended Schooling in the context of improving school performance
2012	Hayfield awarded further work across Farrington LA
2012	Gadley's Extended Schools Manager starts to work nationally with schools on use of Extended Schools to improve standards – framed with the language of the Coalition's school improvement agenda
2014	Phase two of research concludes
2014	Further analysis of data from phases one and two

References

Ainley, P. (2001) 'From a national system locally administered to a national system nationally administered: The new Leviathan in education and training in England'. *Journal for Social Policy*, 30 (3), 457–76.

Anning, A., Cottrell, D., Frost, N., Green, J., and Robinson, M. (2006) *Developing Multiprofessional Teamwork for Integrated Services: Research, policy and practice*. Maidenhead: Open University Press.

Apple, M. (2001) *Educating the 'Right' Way: Markets, standards, god and inequality*. London: Routledge.

— (2004) *Ideology and Curriculum*. London: Routledge.

— (2009) *Global Crises, Social Justice, and Education*. London: Routledge.

Ball, S. (2013) *The Education Debate*. 2nd ed. Bristol: Policy Press.

Barker, R. (ed.) (2009) *Making Sense of Every Child Matters*. Bristol: Policy Press.

BBC (2014) 'Walsall Council warns of job cuts and library closures'. Online. www.bbc.co.uk/news/uk-england-birmingham-29694325 (accessed 19 June 2015).

BBC (2014) 'Thatcher explored education overhaul'. Online. www.bbc.co.uk/news/uk-30625941 (accessed 19 June 2015).

Bergstrom, Y., and Wahlstrom, N. (2008) 'A reformed upper secondary school: With what ambitions?' *Education and Democracy*, 17 (1), 15–26.

Blair, T. (1999) 'Speech by the Prime Minister Tony Blair about Education Action Zones'. Online. http://tna.europarchive.org/20030731055620/http:/www.pm.gov.uk:80/output/Page1172.asp (accessed 19 June 2015).

— (2010) *A Journey*. London: Hutchinson.

Broadhead, P. and Martin, D. (2009) 'Education and Every Child Matters'. In Barker, R. (ed.) *Making Sense of Every Child Matters*. Bristol: Policy Press.

Brown, W. (2006) 'American nightmare: Neoliberalism, neoconservatism, and de-democratization'. *Political Theory*, 34, 390–414.

Cambridge County Council (1976) *Report of the Education Committee*. Cambridge.

Cameron, D. (2009) speech to the Conservative Party Annual Conference, 8 October, Manchester.

Campbell, A., and Martin, D. (2011) 'Every Child Matters: New ethical challenges arising in school'. In Campbell, A., and Broadhead, P. (eds) *Working with Children and Young People: Ethical debates and practices across disciplines and continents*. Oxford: Peter Lang, 37–57.

Carpenter, H., Peters, M., Oseman, D., Papps, I., Dyson, A., Jones, L., Cummings, C., Laing, K., and Todd, L. (2012) *Extended Services Evaluation: End of year one report*. London: DfE.

Central Advisory Council for Education (1967) *Children and Their Primary Schools (The Plowden Report)*. London: HMSO.

Chamberlain, T., Rutt, S., and Fletcher-Campbell, F. (2006) *Admissions: Who Goes Where? Messages from the statistics*. Slough: NFER.

References

Children Workforce Development Council (2009) *Progress Towards Integrated Working: 2007/2008 evaluation*. Leeds: CWDC. Online. http://dera.ioe.ac.uk/10514/ (accessed 2 August 2016).

Chitty, C. (2011) 'A massive power grab from local communities: The real significance of the 2010 White Paper and the 2011 Education Bill'. *Forum for promoting 3–19 comprehensive education*, 53 (1), 11–14.

Clarke, J., and Newman, J. (1997) *The Managerial State: Power, politics and ideology in the remaking of social welfare*. London: Sage.

Coalition for Community Schools (2014) *Reports*. Online. www.communityschools.org/policy_advocacy/default.aspx (accessed 19 June 2015).

Cummings, C., Dyson, A., Papps, I., Pearson, D., Raffo, C., Tiplady, L., and Todd, L. (2006) *Evaluation of the Full Service Schools Initiative, Second Year: Thematic papers*. London: DfES.

Cummings, C., Dyson, A., and Todd, L. (2011) *Beyond the School Gates: Can full service and extended schools overcome disadvantage?* Abingdon: Routledge.

Department for Children, Schools and Families (2007a) *The Children's Plan: Building brighter futures*. London: DCSF.

— (2007b) *Extended Schools: Building on experience*. London: HMSO.

— (2008) *The 21st century school system*. London: DCSF.

— (2010) *Extended Schools National Conference*. London: DCSF.

Department for Education (2010) *The Importance of Teaching*. London: DfE. Online. www.gov.uk/government/uploads/system/uploads/attachment_data/file/175429/CM-7980.pdf (accessed 2 August 2016).

Department for Education and Employment (1998) *Sure Start Local Programmes*. London: DfEE.

— (1999) *Schools Plus: Building learning communities*. London: DfEE. Online. http://dera.ioe.ac.uk/5589/ (accessed 2 August 2016).

Department of Education and Science/Welsh Office (1977) *A New Partnership for Our Schools: Report of the committee of enquiry (The Taylor Report)*. London: HMSO.

Department for Education and Skills (2002) *Full Service Extended Schools: Providing opportunities and services for all*. London: DfES.

— (2003) Green Paper: *Every Child Matters*. London: DfES.

— (2005) *Extended Schools: Access to opportunities and services for all: a prospectus*. London: DfES.

— (2006) *Extended Services Core Offer*. London: DfES.

Donnachie, I. (2000) *Robert Owen: Owen of New Lanark and New Harmony*. East Linton: Tuckwell Press.

Dryfoos, J. (1998) *A Look at Community Schools in 1998*. New York: National Center for Schools and Communities.

— (2002) 'PARTNERING – Full-service community schools: Creating new institutions'. *Phi Delta Kappan*, 83 (5), 393.

Eisenhower Foundation (2005) *Full Service Community Schools Handbook*. Online. www.eisenhowerfoundation.org/docs/FSCS_Handbook_2005.pdf (accessed 19 June 2015).

Eisenstadt, N. (2011) *Providing a Sure Start: How government discovered early childhood*. Bristol: Policy Press.

References

Facer, K. (2011) *Learning Futures: Education, technology and social change*. Abingdon: Routledge.

Field, F. (2011) *The Foundation Years: Preventing poor children becoming poor adults*. London: HMSO.

Fielding, M., and Moss, P. (2011) *Radical Democratic Education and the Common School: A democratic alternative*. Abingdon: Routledge.

Franklin, G. (2009) *Inner London Schools 1918–1944: A thematic study*. Portsmouth: English Heritage.

Frost, N. (2005) *Professionalism, Partnership and Joined-Up Thinking: A research review of front-line working with children and families*. Sheffield: Research in Practice.

Garratt, D., and Forrester, G. (2012) *Education Policy Unravelled*. London: Bloomsbury.

Giddens, A. (1998) *The Third Way: The renewal of social democracy*. Cambridge: Polity Press.

Gove, M. (2010) 'Education: questions and answer session'. 15 November. London: Hansard.

— (2011) speech to the Conservative Party National Conference. Manchester, 4 October.

The Guardian (2014) 'National Archives: revelations from released documents'. 30 December. Online. www.theguardian.com/uk-news/2014/dec/30/national-archives-revelations-released-documents (accessed 2 August 2016).

— (2015) 'It's a political failure: How Sweden's celebrated schools system fell into crisis'. 10 June. Online. www.theguardian.com/world/2015/jun/10/sweden-schools-crisis-political-failure-education (accessed 19 June 2015).

Hargreaves, D. (2010) *Creating a Self-improving School System*. Nottingham: NCSL.

Harlem Children's Zones (2014) http://hcz.org/ (accessed 19 June 2015).

HM Government (2010) 'Plans to encourage troops to become teachers'. Online. www.gov.uk/government/news/plans-to-encourage-troops-to-become-teachers (accessed 19 June 2015).

Howlett, J. (2013) *Progressive Education: A critical introduction*. London: A&C Black.

Jeffs, T. (1999) *Henry Morris, Village Colleges, Community Education and the Ideal Order*. Ticknall: Educational Heretics Press.

Johansson, I., and Moss, P. (2010) 'Re-forming the school: Taking Swedish lessons'. *Children and Society*, 26 (1), 25–36.

Labour Party (1997) *General Election Manifesto: Because Britain deserves better*. London.

Local Government Association (2014) *Future Funding Outlook 2014*. London: Local Government Association.

Martin, D. (2012) 'Schools and children and young people's services have successfully constructed local, holistic, multi-professional partnerships: But what's next under the Coalition government?' BERA national conference. Manchester, September.

References

— (2014) 'Young people, education, families and communities: Marginalised hopes and dreams?' In Harrison, R., and Sanders, T. (eds) *Social Policies and Social Control: New perspectives on the 'not so big society'*. Bristol: Policy Press, 101–15.

Martin, D., and Dunhill, A. (2013) 'Contemporary policy: Children and young people's workforce in crisis as schools are directed to return to so called traditional educational values'. Online. http://tinyurl.com/z5lyqdv (accessed 2 August 2016).

Midwinter, E. (1973) *Patterns of Community Education*. London: Ward Lock.

Mongon, D., and Leadbeater, C. (2012) *School Leadership for Public Value: Understanding valuable outcomes for children, families and communities*. London: IOE.

Morris, H. (1924) *The Village College: Being a memorandum on the provision of educational and social facilities for the countryside, with special reference to Cambridgeshire*. Cambridge: Cambridge University.

Mortimore, P. (2013) *Education Under Siege: Why there is a better alternative*. Bristol: Policy Press.

Moss, P. (2010) 'We cannot continue as we are: The educator in an education for survival'. *Contemporary Issues in Early Childhood*, 11 (1), 8–19.

Moss, P., and Haydon, G. (2008) 'Every Child Matters and the concept of education'. *Viewpoint*, 17. Institute of Education.

Ohlsson, J. (2004) *Arbetslag och lärande* [Working Team and Learning Processes]. Lund: *Studentlitteratur*.

Piper, J. (2006) *Schools Plus to Extended Schools*. Coventry: ContinYou.

Power, S., and Whitty, G. (1999) 'New Labour's education policy: First, second or third way?' *Journal of Education Policy*, 14 (5), 535–46.

Save the Children (2012) *Developing Children's Zones for England*. London: Save the Children. Online. www.savethechildren.org.uk/sites/default/files/docs/Developing-Childrens-Zones.pdf (accessed 2 August 2016).

— (2013) *Developing Children's Zones for England: What's the evidence?* London: Save the Children.

Shamir, R. (2008) 'The age of responsibilization: On market-embedded morality'. *Economy and Society*, 37 (1), 1–19.

Social Exclusion Unit (1998) *Bringing Britain Together: A national strategy for neighbourhood renewal*. London: HMSO.

— (2001) *National Strategy for Neighbourhood Renewal: Policy Action Team Audit*. London: Cabinet Office.

UK Parliament (2004) Children Act 2004. London: HMSO.

United States Department for Education (2001) *No Child Left Behind*. Online. http://www2.ed.gov/nclb/landing.jhtml (accessed 19 June 2015).

Varlas, L. (2008) *Full Service Community Schools*. Online. www.ascd.org/publications/newsletters/policy_priorities/summer08/num54/full/Full-Service_Community_Schools.aspx (accessed 19 June 2015).

Whalen, S. (2007) 'Three Years into Chicago's Community Schools Initiative (CSI): Progress, challenges, and lessons learned'. Online. www.aypf.org/documents/CSI_ThreeYearStudy.pdf (accessed 19 June 2015).

Whitty, G. (2002) *Making Sense of Education Policy: Studies in the sociology and politics of education*. London: Sage.

References

Wiborg, S. (2010) 'Swedish Free Schools: Do they work?' LLAKES Research Paper 18. London: Centre for Learning and Life Chances in Knowledge Economies and Societies, Institute of Education. Online. www.llakes.org/wp-content/uploads/2010/09/Wiborg-online.pdf (accessed 2 August 2016).

Wilshaw, M. (2012) *The Report of HM Chief Inspector of Education, Children's Services and Skills 2011–12,* London: HMSO.

Winlow, S., and Hall, S. (2013) *Rethinking Social Exclusion: The end of the social?* London: Sage.

Index

1870 Education Act   10
1988 Education Reform Act   3, 6, 9, 13–15, 19, 30
1944 Education Act   10
2010 General Election   45

academies   xi, 16, 22, 46, 51, 57, 67, 68, 76, 130, 156; programme   22
academization   46, 51, 67, 71, 72, 125, 129, 140; programme   71, 72
academy   5, 34, 46, 48, 51, 52, 57, 66, 67, 71, 72, 125, 129, 152, 156
adult education   19, 35, 55, 80, 91, 110, 142
anti-social behaviour   98, 100, 105, 134
autonomy   2, 3, 14, 19, 22, 65, 102

before and after school club   49, 78, 100
Blair, Tony   16–18, 22
Brown, Gordon   4, 13, 68

Cabinet Office   18
Callaghan, James   10–12, 16
Campus Facilitator   136, 137, 139–41, 143–7
central government   3, 12, 13, 16, 17, 19, 22, 27, 32, 41, 73, 77, 81, 87, 115, 130, 132–5, 140, 142, 147–9
Change for Children   2, 151
Charter Schools   24
Chicago schools   25
Children's Centres   xii, 23, 59
Children's Minister   2, 4, 18, 20, 21, 132, 134, 152, 153
Children's Plan   4, 20, 21, 64, 129, 152, 158
Children's Social Care   33, 39-41, 43–5, 48, 49, 56, 60, 62, 63, 79, 80, 85, 99, 100, 101, 106, 119, 122, 144
Children's Trusts   19, 152
Children's Zones   26, 27, 158–60
church-led research   38, 48, 117
Coalition   5–7, 10, 21–5, 27, 30–2, 34, 46, 51, 55, 57, 66–8, 71, 76, 82, 86, 91, 106, 125, 127, 129
Coalition for Community Schools   24, 25
collectivist   13, 15
commissioners   44, 106, 124, 125
Common Assessment Framework (CAF)   41, 43, 49, 50, 137, 148
community divide   70; engagement   93, 98, 115, 118, 155; enterprise   26, 80, 82; events   50, 101; survey   94, 99; survey audit   58, 117, 155
community-based organizations   25, 26, 32, 49, 52, 96, 98, 105, 118, 120, 127; professionals   60; workers   118

community-orientated   25, 26, 59, 77, 88, 138
conflict   44, 64, 70, 72, 103, 113, 115, 122, 124, 126, 129
Connexions strategy   1
cradle to career   26

deficit model   1, 52, 141, 143
Department for Children, Schools and Families   20
Department for Education   xii, 4, 21
disadvantaged communities   9, 11, 12, 16, 17, 19, 23, 24, 26, 30, 91, 102, 110, 135

early intervention   1, 2, 45, 63, 73, 77, 80, 84, 88, 100, 144
Early Years   40, 42, 49, 50, 56, 62, 97, 138, 142, 144, 155
education-in-its-broadest-sense   xiii
Education Action Zones (EAZs)   12, 17
Education Priority Areas (EPAs)   11
Excellence in Cities   35, 37
Extended Schools Core Offer   8, 20, 21, 80, 82, 110, 119, 125, 145, 152

faith worker   42
family-based services   33
family support   45, 59, 63, 64, 79, 80, 100, 122, 133; workers   59, 64
free market   13
free schools   xi, 22, 27, 28, 30, 46
Full Service Extended School   xi, 2, 6, 9, 18, 19, 91–5, 101–3, 107, 110, 115, 128, 151, 154
Full Service Schools   3, 23–6, 76, 85, 92–7, 151

Gadley community and schools   53
General Practitioners (GPs)   2, 79
Gove, Michael   1, 21, 22
governance arrangements   xiii, 10, 24, 39, 40, 48, 49, 61, 64, 83, 91, 93, 118–20, 151

Harlem Children's Zone   26
Hayfield community and schools   73
health services   10, 11, 33, 44, 55, 56, 66, 85
holistic   21, 27, 36, 51, 52, 65, 73, 85, 87, 88, 106, 107, 121, 123, 144, 148

inner city   1, 11, 12, 33, 73, 74, 85, 87, 110, 143, 156; schools   87, 88, 126, 156

'joined-up working'   2, 18
'joined-up thinking'   2, 18

LA Children's Plan   62, 129
LA leaders   44
Learning Support Unit (LSU)   37, 38, 47
Local Authority   xi, 2–4, 56, 73, 74, 90, 151
Local Education Authorities (LEAs)   10, 11, 13, 16
Local Management of Schools   13

162

Index

market failures 142
market place xi, 14, 15, 111, 112, 116
middle managers 2, 155
missed opportunities 49
Morris, Henry 11
multi-professional working 41, 45, 51, 63, 78, 80, 81, 100, 113, 130, 152, 156
multi-purpose institutions xi
mutual learning 49, 105, 122, 126; understandings 49, 108, 120, 122, 123–6, 134
mutual professionalism 8, 105, 108, 120, 121, 124, 126–9, 135, 140, 141, 144–9; localized 8, 124, 126–9, 135, 142

National College of School Leadership 6, 69
National Curriculum xi, 13, 105
National Strategy for Neighbourhood Review 1999 17
neoconservatism xi
neoconservative 7, 8, 9, 12–16, 22, 23, 30, 109, 131, 132, 142, 143, 149
neoliberal 5, 8, 9, 12, 13, 15, 16, 22, 23, 30, 108, 131, 132, 142, 143, 149
neoliberalism 7, 12, 13, 15, 131, 136
new professionalism 50, 51, 104, 126, 132, 143
New Right 7, 9, 10, 12, 14, 16, 21, 22, 23
Newtown community and schools 89
No Child Left Behind 24

Ofsted xi, 13, 14, 34, 35, 38, 46, 55, 56, 69, 75, 82, 86–9, 91, 92, 94, 98, 105, 115, 121
Orpintown community and schools 33
out of school care 28
outside influencers 134
Owen, Robert 10
ownership 36, 48, 56, 80, 82, 98, 144, 146, 148, 156; collective 38

Parent Teacher Association (PTA) 55, 57
parenting support 3, 19, 26, 79
partial understandings 50, 52, 103, 107, 115, 118, 121–3, 126, 141
partnership working 36, 39, 40, 44, 47, 67, 98, 99, 106, 109, 110, 113, 114, 125, 129
performativity 38, 40, 44, 47, 67, 98, 99, 106, 109, 110, 113, 114, 125, 129
pipeline 26
Plowden Report 11
Primary Care Trust (PCT) 33, 44, 50, 55, 64, 65, 71, 81, 106, 124, 125
professional perspective 107,122
progressive universalism 18, 22, 131, 143, 151
pseudo-market 1, 14, 17, 20, 115, 149
Pupil Premium 141

Reagan, Ronald 12
Ruskin speech 10, 12

Save the Children 26, 27
school leadership 6, 20, 36, 47, 67, 69, 81, 84, 95, 102, 104, 113, 115, 123, 134; improvement 9, 24, 66, 83, 87, 92–5, 101–3, 110, 114, 115, 154, 156; nurse 65, 118; performance 1, 20, 63, 76, 87, 88, 91, 102; trusts 56; workforce 58, 69, 102, 112–19, 123, 127
schools coming together 8, 41, 67, 108, 109, 116, 120
Schools Plus 18, 27, 151
SEN 36–8, 47, 48, 113, 117, 141
sense of mutuality 47, 145
social capital 94, 102
Social Exclusion Unit 17
sports events 63, 100
Standardised Assessment Testing (SATs) 13, 23, 91, 110
strategic leaders 2, 50, 66
Sure Start Local Programmes 1, 17
Swedish schooling 27, 28
system leaders 20

teacher training 85, 114
teamworking 29
Thatcher, Margaret 11, 12, 70
'The Importance of Teaching' 23
Third Way 17
'through school' 89, 91
town hall 129
'traditional educational values' 1, 5, 7, 21, 22, 51, 71, 86, 125, 127, 130, 152
transformational change 125–8, 132–4
Troops for Teachers 22
twenty-first-century school 3, 4, 12, 20, 21, 50, 69, 81, 152

unemployment 8, 11, 14, 34, 54, 55, 74, 90, 101
universalism 9
USA 7, 10, 12–14, 16, 23–7, 30, 33, 39, 56, 76, 83, 95, 97, 118, 139

voluntary sector 33, 39, 56, 76, 83, 95, 97, 118, 139

Youth Service 22, 33, 39, 49, 55, 56, 59, 61, 76, 124, 155
youth work 41, 42, 50, 58, 60, 63, 65, 99, 103
youth worker 60, 65, 77, 144

163